*The State of Mind Called Beautiful*

# *the* state *of* mind called beautiful

## SAYADAW U PANDITA

*edited by*
KATE WHEELER

*translated by*
VENERABLE VIVEKANANDA

*forewords by*
JAKE DAVIS AND ANDREW SCHEFFER

Wisdom

Wisdom Publications
199 Elm Street
Somerville, MA 02144 USA
www.wisdompubs.org



An earlier version of the foreword by Jake Davis first appeared in *Buddhadharma* magazine, and is reprinted courtesy of the author.

*Library of Congress Cataloging-in-Publication Data*
Names: Sayadaw, U Pandita, 1921– author. | Wheeler, Kate, 1955– editor. | Vivekananda, Venerable, translator.
Title: The state of mind called beautiful / by Sayadaw U Pandita; edited by Kate Wheeler; translated by Venerable Vivekananda.
Description: Expanded and revised edition. | Somerville, MA: Wisdom Publications, 2017. | Translated from Burmese. | Includes bibliographical references and index. |
Identifiers: LCCN 2017009060 (print) | LCCN 2017027093 (ebook) | ISBN 9781614294566 (ebook) | ISBN 1614294569 (ebook) | ISBN 9781614294313 (pbk.: alk. paper)
Subjects: LCSH: Spiritual life—Buddhism. | Vipaśyanā (Buddhism) | Theravāda Buddhism—Doctrines.
Classification: LCC BQ4302 (ebook) | LCC BQ4302 .S29 2017 (print) | DDC 294.3/444—dc23
LC record available at https://lccn.loc.gov/2017009060

ISBN 978-1-61429-431-3 ebook ISBN 978-1-61429-456-6

21 20 19 18 17
5 4 3 2 1

Cover design by David Ter-Avanesyan/Ter33Design. Cover image © incomible/123RF
Interior design by Gopa & Ted2, Inc. Set in DiacriticalGaramond 11.8/15.3.

Wisdom Publications' books are printed on acid-free paper and meet the guidelines for permanence and durability set by the Council of Library Resources.

This book was produced with environmental mindfulness. For more information, please visit wisdompubs.org/wisdom-environment.

Printed in the United States of America.

MIX
Paper from responsible sources
FSC® C005010
www.fsc.org

Please visit fscus.org.

*Contents*

# *Foreword*

## Sayādaw U Paṇḍita and His Impact

*by Jake Davis*

When Sayādaw U Paṇḍita came to the Insight Meditation Society in Barre, Massachusetts, in 1984, most there knew him then only as the successor to the Mahāsi Sayādaw, who had passed away two years earlier. Yet for many of those who are the most senior teachers in the West today, that retreat provided a singular opportunity to do long-term intensive practice with one whom they came to regard as a true master.

When I was training with him decades later, U Paṇḍita pulled out photo albums from that retreat. I remember his joyous smile as he showed me pictures of Joseph Goldstein, Sharon Salzberg, Jack Kornfield, and others, glowing from months of intensive practice and of course looking a good bit younger than I remembered them. Over the course of this and subsequent retreats held in the United States, Australia, and elsewhere, many of these Western teachers describe not only training in *satipaṭṭhāna* (mindfulness meditation) practice with a level of energy and precision beyond what they had previously imagined possible, but also for the first time engaging in intensive long-term practice of the *brahma vihāras*: mettā, compassion, sympathetic joy, and equanimity. The profound impact of this pairing—U Paṇḍita's precise energetic style of mindfulness practice with brahmavihāra practice—on the way in which Buddhist meditation is taught in the West is abundantly evident. However, it is not always clear to newer students how many contemporary Western presentations are in large part a legacy of U Paṇḍita's formative guidance of a generation of Western teachers.

U Paṇḍita was born in Burma in 1921. Losing his mother at age four and his father at ten, he began his primary education in the traditional way, at a monastery, and ordained as a novice monk when he was twelve. At eighteen, he went to study with the great Sayādaw U Kelasa of the Kyauk Tan Mahabodhi Monastery near Bago and ordained as a *bhikkhu* there at twenty. U Paṇḍita would go on to become a distinguished scholar of the Pāḷi texts in his own right, teaching textual studies in Rangoon, earning the preeminent title of Abhivaṃsa, and eventually participating, when he was thirty-three, as both reciter and corrector of Pāḷi in the Sixth Sangha Council of 1956.

While teaching Pāḷi in Rangoon in his late twenties, U Paṇḍita also studied English with Saya-gyi U Hpe Thin, and the two of them made an agreement that whoever came to see Dhamma first would tell the other. Saya-gyi U Hpe Thin later went to practice at the newly established center run by the Mahāsi Sayādaw and, becoming satisfied with his practice and inspired by the teaching there, U Hpe Thin encouraged the young U Paṇḍita to go along as well. Thus it was that at twenty-nine, U Paṇḍita took up the practice of satipaṭṭhāna as taught by the Mahāsi Sayādaw. He too became inspired by the practice and eager to share this taste of Dhamma with relatives, friends, and others. Through his own experience, U Paṇḍita had also become firmly convinced that textual study of the Buddha's teachings needed to be complemented by practical application of meditation practice.

On the strength of this realization, when he was thirty-four, U Paṇḍita left his post teaching Pāḷi textual studies to take up the duties assigned to him by the Mahāsi Sayādaw. He guided yogis for over three decades at the Rangoon center, including many of the Burmese monks who would go on to become leading teachers of the Mahāsi method in their own right. In addition, a handful of young Westerners such as Alan Clements and Steven Smith came to the center in the early 1980s and practiced under the guidance of U Paṇḍita. It was in large part on the strength of the recommendation of these young Westerners that U Paṇḍita was invited to the Insight Meditation Society in 1984 to conduct that historic retreat, which would prove to be a major watershed in the training of Western teachers of mindfulness meditation.

In 1979, at age fifty-seven, U Paṇḍita was appointed as a guiding Nayaka teacher at the Mahāsi center and with the passing of the Mahāsi Sayādaw in 1982 was appointed to the lead role of Ovadacariya at the center. He served in that role for eight years, then left to found the Panditarama Shwe Taung Gon Center. The new center flourished, and many branch centers were eventually established under his guidance in Burma and around the world. In addition to training many thousands of meditators in his precise, rigorous style of practice, U Paṇḍita dedicated himself to the training of female Anagarika nuns from Nepal, Burma, the United States, and elsewhere, in both textual study and meditative practice to the highest standards. The immense potential of this contribution to the strength of the Buddha's teachings in the West is only beginning to be felt.

While his mastery of meditation practice is widely recognized, it is less emphasized in the West how U Paṇḍita embodied and insisted on the purity of one's morality as a foundational and essential means of avoiding suffering for oneself and others. One Burmese monk, now an elder, recalls that when he lived as a young novice under U Paṇḍita, the novices did not dare to so much as *look* at the nuns, much less chat with them. Yet this strict observance of *sīla*, which U Paṇḍita held himself to as well, was motivated by a compassionate understanding of the suffering that can follow from a failure to do so. As the American teacher Michele McDonald relates, it was the great strength of U Paṇḍita's sīla that made her feel safe enough to trust him as a guide through very difficult aspects of practice.

For all his many personal strengths, U Paṇḍita tried to include in his teaching as little of himself as possible. American nun and long-time student Daw Vajiranani recalls U Paṇḍita telling her that the Buddha's teachings recorded in the Pāḷi texts should be given first priority, next the commentaries, and after that the lineage of teachers down to the present; one's own views and innovations should carry the least weight. For this reason, U Paṇḍita emphasized that in order to guide others skillfully, a meditation teacher needs careful study of the Pāḷi texts, just as textual study must also be completed by practical application of these teachings in meditative practice. Throughout his own teaching career, U Paṇḍita never forgot his great debt to his own teacher, the Mahāsi Sayādaw. And he emphasized Mahāsi's immense contribution in making clear how the Pāḷi suttas, beginning from the Buddha's first teaching in the *Dhammacakkappavattana Sutta*, offer precise practical guidance for meditation practice.

Sayādaw U Paṇḍita will be remembered as embodying the aspiration to pass on, intact, the purity of the lineage of teaching from the Buddha that he had received. His remarkable energy for this kind of service made him one of the foremost meditation masters of our time and kept him traveling widely and giving daily talks until his final weeks in the spring of 2016. His passing truly represents the end of an era.

JAKE DAVIS studied and practiced under the guidance of Sayādaw U Paṇḍita for nearly a decade, both as a layperson and as a monk. He has taught with Vipassana Hawaii and at Brown University, and holds a research position at New York University.

# *Foreword*

## A Personal Reflection on Sayādaw U Paṇḍita
*by Andrew Scheffer*

I first met Sayādaw U Paṇḍita in 1991 when I was twenty-two years old. At that time, I spent two months ordained as a temporary monk in my first long intensive retreat. Through the daily talks, the short group interviews, and one-to-one meetings, it became obvious to me that Sayādaw-*gyi*, as he was often affectionally called by those close to him, was a great being and that I could learn a lot from spending as much time with him as possible.

In fact, because of his special qualities—great clarity and enthusiasm for the Buddhist teachings, and emphasis on mindfulness practice—I sought him out repeatedly and spent what turned out to be twenty-five years in close contact with him. I traveled to see him regularly, usually for up to several months a year. This included years in silent retreat under his guidance, but also, after many years of practice, I was able to serve as a *kappiya*, or attendant. As you can see in this book, Sayādaw-gyi had an incredible ability to talk about the Dhamma not just from theory, but in a way that really brings topics to life. And *The State of Mind Called Beautiful* includes what I regard as the most inspiring talk on the qualities of the Buddha that I have heard among the thousands of talks he has given.

It is really quite amazing that these talks Sayādaw-gyi gave many years ago still come to life so vividly even today. This is also uplifting and encouraging—especially in light of his recent passing.

Sayādaw-gyi did not try to "improve upon" the Buddhist teachings using his own words, but instead always used explanations found within the classical texts themselves. In this way, Sayādaw-gyi was the ultimate student of the Buddha, holding the Buddha and the Buddha's words in the highest esteem. And he continued to reflect on and study the Buddha's teachings, setting a compelling example for us to follow—as he did through all his leadership. Moreover, he always set the highest standard for himself, only asking us to do what he had done, or what he himself was trying to do himself. A person of great humility, Sayādaw-gyi had no desire to become popular and famous or leave his own mark, he merely tried to pass on this body of knowledge of Buddha's teaching effectively and as flawlessly as he could.

Throughout the years that I knew him, in addition to introducing him to my family and friends, I invited the US Ambassador to Singapore to meet him as I did several famous Tibetan rinpoches. I also had the opportunity to be present when Aung San Suu Kyi came to visit Sayādaw-gyi to ask for guidance with some leadership issues she was facing for Myanmar. Sayādaw-gyi was regularly giving guidance to world leaders—and always used the teachings of the Buddha to do so. From his visit to the cosmopolitan bustle of New York City to his final moments in a hospital bed, I never saw Sayādaw-gyi affected by anger or greed. His accomplishment of mind—uprooting the very causes of suffering—was simply not impacted by worldly conditions.

Recently, a few of his closest disciples had the opportunity to look at some of his notes for Dhamma talks, and it became clear how incredibly brief they always were, simply an outline of key points. The details and examples he used in talks—and that appear in this book—were all brought forth spontaneously, based upon his own knowledge and the needs of the audience. His talks were works of genius. (And by the way, his talks have been recorded extensively for posterity and are available online freely for you to see for yourself).

The more we listen to or study Sayādaw-gyi's rendition of the Buddha's teachings, the more we realize their splendor. I remember that at one point, Sayādaw-gyi asked me how much of his talks I thought I could fully understand. Truthfully, at that time, I could only comprehend 35 percent—and I had been following and studying with him for decades! It was usually the newer students or those with less understanding who thought they could understand everything he said—not differentiating between simply hearing and really comprehending.

With those who spent extensive time beyond retreat with Sayādaw-gyi, he was almost always lighthearted and fun-loving. Sometimes I teased him that though his reputation was that of a lion, I found him more like a cat. Yet, for those closest to him, we also responded quickly and respectfully to the best of our ability when Sayādaw directed us to correct an error or overcome a shortcoming—as he often did, for our benefit.

When Sayādaw-gyi was nearby, I felt like I was experiencing miracles. Not through any outward display but simply through his lightness of heart and his ability to help me find peace of mind and redirect my attention wisely, no matter which worldly circumstances I confronted. No matter what challenges life threw at me, Sayādaw-gyi helped me to see them in a new light and regain the energy and motivation to move forward and bring my practice fully to bear once again. He knew we would fail and fall, again and again, would continue to make mistakes—and he always was the first to support us and encourage us to get back on our feet.

Sayādaw-gyi gave tirelessly of himself until his last breath, in April 2016—having been a monk for more than seventy-five years, and having guided thousands upon thousands of students, in both the East and West. Here, in *The State of Mind Called Beautiful,* I hope Sayādaw-gyi's teachings provide inspiration and clear guidance for you!

ANDREW SCHEFFER first met Sayādaw U Paṇḍita when Andrew was twenty-two. He studied closely with him for the next twenty-five years as both a layman and monk, training for over ten thousand hours in silent meditation retreats. Andrew currently teaches meditation at corporations and to individuals—dividing his time between Southern California and the New York metro area. Andrew continues to visit Myanmar regularly.

## *Editor's Preface*

The talks in this book were given at a one-month retreat in May 2003 inaugurating the Forest Refuge, the long-term retreat facility at Insight Meditation Society in Barre, Massachusetts. Sayādaw U Paṇḍita was eighty-two at the time. When he died in Bangkok this past April, 2016, at ninety-five, it was as if the earth trembled. We lost a titan, a giant of Dhamma. For me, like many others, he was a kind and loving father or grandfather, the one who taught us precisely how we could tame our minds.

Yes, he could be intimidating, awe-inspiring, stern. He was famous for not lowering his newspaper during your interview if he felt you were reporting opinions and mental proliferation instead of direct experiences. His talks are full of criticism for "recidivists" and "chronic meditators" who attend retreat after retreat without making the effort necessary for achieving liberation. He liked to use words like *crush, destroy, capture, attack, pierce,* and *uproot.* "No compassion whatsoever for the defilements of the mind," was his advice. Yet Sayādaw-gyi (as he's affectionately known—"Great, great teacher") was also tender, funny, unswervingly loyal to the principle of freedom. Your freedom. Since only you can uproot your suffering, and you also tend to get distracted from the task, he was there to get you back on track.

Unswervingly. So, upon hearing of his death, in addition to the loss, I was surprised—and surprised to be surprised. After all, wasn't he old? And didn't he teach students to know, most intimately, that a human being is nothing but a stream of impermanent, impersonal phenomena? Yet Sayādaw-gyi had seemed changeless.

I'd been skeptical when we first met. Thanks, in part, to Western cultural history and education, I'd felt his certitude must be no better than hidebound dogma. Indeed, Sayādaw-gyi was a traditionalist who trusted his method implicitly, and believed in striving for a goal. After knowing him for nearly forty years, practicing under him, studying him from various distances and angles, I'd now say Sayādaw-gyi's character was based on a similarly unshakable internal knowing. It gave him extraordinary power as a teacher and leader; a kind of ruthlessness about discarding what was trivial.

His visits to the United States and the books that emerged fundamentally altered the way vipassanā meditation is taught and practiced in the West. His first visit, in 1984, when he was sixty-three, electrified the founders and senior teachers of the Insight tradition in the United States, Australia, and Europe. Talks from this retreat became his book *In This Very Life*, a road map for Dhamma practice as seen through the lens of the Mahāsi style of meditation. *In This Very Life* describes the methods, the early stages, and pitfalls of what's called the progress of insight. In the Mahāsi tradition, the progress of insight is considered a sine qua non for overcoming the tortures of the mind, and it is a direct path to *nibbāna*, the unconditioned. The progress consists of an orderly series of altered perceptions, which arise in the course of that method of practice. (Note that the Progress is a *process,* and it's easy to misinterpret, especially if you're trying to assess yourself. It also doesn't work the same with every person. So it's best to sign up for a retreat with an experienced teacher who can give you specific guidance).

At the 2003 retreat, Sayādaw-gyi brought with him two younger teaching monks, one Burmese and one German, to provide the consistent frequent interviews the Mahāsi method demands. There were also two nuns, one Burmese and one from the United States, who were being trained as teachers, along with a lay translator from the United States. When this phalanx walked into the Dharma hall on the first night, Sayādaw-gyi's purposefulness was unmistakable. I recall sitting on my cushion thinking, as of a rock band, "They came to play," and resolving to meet them with my own best effort.

As usual, the retreatants ranged from seasoned Buddhist teachers to a first-timer who'd never done a night of retreat before, but had unexpectedly won the registration lottery and who wore a black leather jacket throughout the retreat. I saw him smoking anxious cigarettes in the forest. But he stuck it out till the end. I sometimes wonder what the long-term effect of that monthlong retreat was for him.

Sayādaw-gyi settled on his monk's throne and cleared his throat to offer the first talk in this volume, speaking in a rapid murmur of Burmese without notes. Clearly he was taking a new approach: this series of talks, which is edited into this volume, would be a broader picture.

The panorama begins with the fundamental teachings. Dhamma (Sanskrit: Dharma), the truth, is what we should do; Vinaya, the discipline, is what we should stop doing. Between the two, our practice is like planting flowers and pulling up weeds. It is necessary to do practices that strengthen the mind and heal societies and families, because violence, war, and instability mark our current days. These practices are called the four guardian meditations. They uplift and protect us, and even long-term retreat meditators are asked to practice them. But inner actions like meditation are not enough. There must be outer, compassionate activity—with no compromise of ethics. The Earth, he said, appears to be in the control of people who "resemble demons more than human beings." Leaders who attempt to control these inhuman beings often sink to the same level themselves. We must resist this, he said. "Compassion," he observed, "says what needs to be said. And wisdom doesn't fear the consequences." At the time, his country was subject to a brutal dictatorship, and Sayādaw-gyi publicly supported democratic reforms at great personal risk to himself.

Next he drilled deep into the fundamental mechanics of how a mind is healed by Dhamma. One of the core teachings of *The State of Mind Called Beautiful* is the exposition of how and why the Noble Eightfold Path is present in every moment of mindfulness. He also systematizes and concretizes the relationship between morality, concentration, and wisdom in ways that any psychoanalyst would admire. Restraint suppresses the physical acting out of impulses. Then outer life is calm, but the tormenting impulses are deeply embedded and likely to remain. Concentration training can divert the mind away from its obsessions. Finally, with sufficient clarity of mind, direct awareness can penetrate to the inherent lack of substance. This is how intuitive wisdom develops and dissolves the pain of the mind.

"The defilements are disgusting, dreadful, fearsome, and frightening," he thunders.

Look around at the world. Ask yourself if this sounds right.

Since the 2003 retreat, the Forest Refuge has housed thousands of meditators and produced billions of moments of mindfulness. There are many waves of influence that have succeeded Sayādaw U Paṇḍita: there's been great interest and scathing criticism of the progress of insight. Online manuals describe details that Mahāsi masters keep hidden lest meditators innocently dupe themselves with inauthentic realizations and stay stuck in concepts that go nowhere. Other online communities critique the progress of insight as dangerous and destabilizing. Wise monk-masters emphasize relaxed, open-field awareness; lay teachers well-versed in deep retreat and also Western psychology advise us to practice kindness first, because a harsh, self-hating mind is very difficult to work with. Usually it's not long before Sayādaw U Paṇḍita's name is invoked, all too often as a self-justifying contrast to whatever technique is being defended at the moment. His methods are called too brutal, not psychologically savvy. Surely some of the critiques are fair enough, but others seem unkind and shallow. He is a legend because he deserves to be. When to be delicate, when to be strong. How to pinpoint experience, how to tell reality from delusion. The skills and clarity he taught are indispensable these days, when the Buddha's starkest teachings about the dangers of samsara are beginning to ring louder than ever before in our lifetime.

With this in mind, we offer you *The State of Mind Called Beautiful.*

Kate Wheeler

# *Author's Preface*

THIS EXPLANATION OF *satipaṭṭhāna vipassanā,* commonly known as insight meditation, is offered in close accordance with the texts—the suttas and commentaries of the Theravadin Buddhist tradition. Many favorable circumstances and interconnections made this book possible. Gratitude must be expressed to many people—the translator, Venerable Sayādaw U Vivekānanda, the editors, donors, volunteers, and employees of Wisdom Publications; the meditators attending the retreat at the Forest Refuge at the Insight Meditation Society in Barre, Massachusetts, where the talks were given in May 2003; the staff and donors of the Forest Refuge; and all readers of this book who are interested in purifying their minds through Dhamma.

May all readers benefit from this book by putting its contents to use.

Sayādaw U Paṇḍita
Hse Mile Gon Forest Center, Bago, Myanmar
January 2006

# *Introduction to Dhamma Vinaya*

THE BUDDHA UNDERSTOOD what is beneficial and what is harmful, what leads to happiness and what increases misery in our lives. Out of compassion he left a teaching and training to increase our happiness and that of all beings. This teaching includes the Dhamma, the beneficial truth about existence; and the Vinaya, the discipline or training. Without a discipline, truth would remain an abstraction, something to talk about rather than to live. Without truth as its basis and goal, discipline would be meaningless. Actually, the Dhamma and Vinaya converge in leading us to happiness, well-being, and genuine fulfillment, and together they establish the only lifestyle that can eradicate suffering.

If we want to be completely free from suffering and help others to be free, we must practice Dhamma Vinaya. This means developing, increasing, and strengthening our realization of the path, drawing out its full potential. Whoever does this will gradually become more pure, cultured, gentle, peaceful, and lovable. Such a person will eventually gain the "special insight," a liberating insight that cuts through and extinguishes mental afflictions. Such a person will truly understand the happiness of which the Buddha speaks.

Those familiar with Buddhist terminology will know that the term *Vinaya* usually refers to the monks' code of conduct, and that Buddhism offers different sets of ethical precepts for monks, nuns, and laypeople. Monks rely on 227 precepts to develop their wholesome volition and support their meditation practice. Nuns can rely on eight or ten, while laypeople generally sustain five basic observances to prevent them from going wrong.

Though this may seem—and is, indeed—contrary to ordinary, worldly ways of thinking, the monks' and nuns' renunciate way of life was designed by the Buddha to be the easiest way to reach genuine happiness and an end to personal suffering.

However, the Buddha taught a complete training of body, speech, and mind that anyone, ordained or not, can undertake successfully. This path of training aims at the complete and permanent removal of all mental issues that torment beings. Moral discipline is the foundation without which this endeavor cannot succeed, but following moral precepts is not itself sufficient to liberate the mind and heart.

Without adding an internal, mental discipline, moreover, not even the most basic of precepts can truly be maintained for very long. For as soon as internal compulsion arises, if there is no inner discipline, then the impulse will be unbearable and problematic action will ensue.

True disciples of the Buddha can be recognized by a healthy form of fear—they are afraid of the inner defilements, for they understand the destructive tendencies inside the mind to be the most dangerous forces in the world, more powerful than any earthquake or tsunami. A true disciple, a true practitioner, recognizes that whenever a person is gripped by greed, hatred, and ignorance, he or she is a danger to himself and others.

Therefore a true disciple of the Buddha can also be recognized by her or his concerted efforts not to succumb to the inner defilements—but rather to see through them, control them, diminish their influence, and eventually to extirpate them once and for all.

Up to the moment of full liberation, everyone is bound to fall away from Dhamma Vinaya again and again, whether they wear monastic robes or ordinary clothing. When and if this happens, one must humbly return to the training: one must sustain and increase one's level of effort, refine one's moral actions, strengthen concentration, and thus promote the arising of wisdom. With such sincere dedication one will come to know the meaning of *vimutti*—liberation, deliverance, inner freedom. The possibility of vimutti is the beauty hidden inside each of our minds. To fulfill that possibility is the maximum expression of value in our human lives.

The traditional path of the monk and the nun remains open and invites all those who, regardless of ethnic origin, nationality, or class, wish to forsake worldly engagements and pursue Dhamma Vinaya in an extraordinary manner. Yet most of you who read this book will be laypeople. I encourage all of you to take to heart what I say here. I am giving my best effort to teach you and I hope you will give your best effort to practice. Then, our connection will have been worthwhile.

# 1 *Overview of the Training*

The Buddha gives clear instructions on how to develop moral behavior, concentrate the mind, and see clearly with insight wisdom. These are called the three trainings; in Pāḷi, *sīla sikkhā, samādhi sikkhā,* and *paññā sikkhā*—the training in morality, the training in concentration, and the training in wisdom. The three trainings should be taken as the meaning of Dhamma Vinaya. The meaning of Dhamma Vinaya is not a verbal one. The meaning will appear inasmuch as it is enacted, experienced, and brought to life within an individual.

The word *sikkhā* means training oneself so that certain qualities arise. If we put in the effort to follow the Buddha's instructions, the results will arise quite naturally and lawfully. This is certain.

Along with the instructions for training, the Buddha and his commentators include detailed explanations of the benefits of Dhamma Vinaya and the disadvantages of not engaging it. These descriptions help us to understand the training, to feel enthusiasm for it, and to reject the habits of an untrained, unskillful mind.

## Examining a Precept

To see how this works, let us examine the first precept of moral behavior for laypeople, the injunction against killing.

The Buddha admonishes us to avoid tormenting and killing all beings whatsoever, even small creatures whose lives may seem insignificant in comparison with our own.

Say a mosquito, ant, or flea bites us. Based on the unpleasant feeling in the body, then *dosa,* or ill will, immediately arises in the mind. If we lack patience and forgiveness, we will surely take revenge in a way that spells disaster for the insect. Buddhist training aims to make us feel repugnance, not only toward our lack of compassion and self-control but also toward its consequences. If we become sensitized to the practice of the precepts and the consequences of breaking them, we will take great care to avoid violence in any of our actions.

As practitioners, the major benefit of refraining from, say, swatting a mosquito is the victory we gain over the internal enemies of anger and ill will. With this victory, we have gained an initial form of *avera,* freedom from enmity. Freedom from enmity, as we will see in detail later on, is equivalent to unconditional or limitless friendliness, *mettā.* Overcoming ill will makes us the protector and friend of all beings, including mosquitoes and ourselves as well, for a mind filled with restraint and compassion is easier to live with than a mind reeking with hate and vengefulness. The harmful consequences of killing are not restricted to the victim. Giving rein to destructive impulses tears apart the mind.

Certain commentarial texts outline further disadvantages of immorality. They list four dangers. First, unless we are psychologically abnormal, if we commit harmful actions we will be plagued by remorse, self-criticism, and self-blame. Second, we risk losing the good opinion of others, especially those wise, kind, and virtuous people whose acceptance we treasure. The texts call this "censure by the wise." Third, if a transgression involves breaking the law we may also face the shame, expense, and inconvenience of punishment by the secular authorities. Last, as a result of our unwholesome volitions, we will endure future difficulties and may even be reborn in a state of loss. (A state of loss, in Buddhist doctrine, means a life where one's mental states are rough and intractable, dense, painful—generally all but impossible to work with. Buddhist cosmology, then, would say that killing sets one up for rebirth as a hell being, a hungry ghost, or an animal; or less drastically, as a person whose life is marked by extreme difficulty.)

Now and in the future, as long as our internal enemies are not appeased, we will be subject to many afflictions. We will have plenty of enemies, we will face all kinds of dangers, and all these will tend to multiply.

## Shame, Dread, and Fear

It may seem surprising, but Buddhist teachings encourage shame, dread, and fear—at least with regard to wrongdoing. Moral shame, called *hiri,* is characterized by disgust or abhorrence toward physical and verbal misconduct. Moral dread or fear, *ottappa,* makes one shrink back from and want to guard oneself against all possible bad behavior. These compunctions are clearly quite interconnected. They are considered to be wholesome and healthy forms of sensitivity. In fact, moral shame and moral dread or fear are respectfully known as "the two guardians of the world."

Yet Buddhist teachings do not suggest we wallow in guilt, recrimination, despair, and worry. These are unproductive, and actually constitute forms of dosa, or hatred, directed toward oneself. Self-hatred is not superior to any other form of hatred and there is no point in indulging it. But moral shame and fear are characterized by a sense of discrimination and decision. One does not feel good about one's harmful actions, but one does not build them into mountains either. Nor does one hide and rationalize them, thus distorting their nature. One example is the alcoholic who claims to be taking a drop to relax, then another and another, until the person ends up passed out on the floor.

The only way to be victorious over the destructive inner forces of the mind is to understand them—and resolve to live in accordance with that knowledge, making sure to do what is needed in order not to repeat them. Let us remember that the kilesas are not personal—they only masquerade as such. If we can see them in a balanced way, not claiming them as "I" or "me" or "mine," yet admitting that we are susceptible to their influence, we will have done a great deal toward keeping them in check.

If on the other hand we don't see any harm in our bad actions and degraded mental states, we obviously won't try to avoid them. Rather, we will indulge them—shamelessly. The texts call such behavior *ahirika* and *anottappa,* "moral shamelessness" and "fearlessness." Please note that this kind of fearlessness is not to be confused with the fearlessness that comes from a liberated understanding, which is an entirely different matter. With vimutti, it is possible to lose one's fear of death, and of unpleasant sensations. But this is very different from moral insensitivity and shamelessness, ahirika and anottappa. These two are present whenever we fail to recognize the disgusting, even terrifying, nature of mental and physical transgressions. At that time our heart and mind are hard, uncaring, and reckless. We don't shrink from hurting ourselves and others. We go ahead and do as we please, impulsively.

Lack of moral sensitivity "chars" and thereby darkens the mind. Just as a person wearing dark-colored clothes absorbs heat on a hot day, a mind charred by ahirika and anottappa absorbs ill will. As the heat of anger, our inner enemy, increases, we fail to recognize the danger of it. We accept the anger, and even support it by forming justifications or blaming others. Our anger then increases. Sooner or later, unless this trend is broken, our rage erupts in some cruel speech or hate-filled action. We will disturb ourselves and our surroundings; we will create agitation, like a violent person who intimidates, injures, and even kills people around him or her. Our virtues fade; moral shame and fear, the guardians of the world, will have been destroyed.

If we can learn not to absorb defilement, and instead to see the danger in it, we will have a strong desire to keep our behavior under mindful control, and we will be motivated to subdue the turbulence of our minds. If the heat of the mental defilements is dispelled, the mind will grow bright, light, and cool. And we, radiant with the virtues of morality, will guard our world.

## Compassion

To guard the world means protecting others just as much as oneself. Compassion, the ability to imagine the pain of others, is implicit in the training of morality.

The Buddha spoke this verse:

> Sabbe tasanti daṇḍassa,
> sabbe bhāyanti maccuno.
> Attānaṃ upamaṃ katvā,
> na haneyya na ghātaye.
>
> All are afraid of the stick,
> all fear death.
> Putting oneself in another's place,
> one should not beat or kill others.

The Buddha evokes the principle of *empathy,* an understanding of how others feel based on one's own experience. All beings fear danger and punishment, all fear death—that is, until they attain one of the two highest stages of liberation, either an *anāgāmī,* a nonreturner; or an arahant, a fully liberated one. Until then, the term *sabbe* refers to us *all,* including oneself.

So, being honest with oneself, one may have to admit that in fact, one may find oneself wishing to torment or injure others somewhat frequently. For most of us, most of the time, these wishes will be subtle, perhaps disguised as a desire to prevail over others, to show them their mistakes.

Often, if we feel we have been wronged, it is not easy to avoid making life difficult for others. We may feel it is important that someone else hears our complaints, and feels badly for all the suffering we have gone through. More grossly, we may fantasize inflicting bodily harm on relative strangers such as politicians, or our "enemies" in other countries—or even within our own country. Many people feel that violent criminals deserve to be executed. And then if someone known to us, close to us, has caused us difficulty, put obstacles in our path, or committed verbal assassination of our character, watch out! We will not be wishing peace upon such people; more likely we will want them to experience some consequences first. If they appear to be happily getting away with what they have done, we may well decide to take matters into our own hands, gaining satisfaction even from petty meannesses such as ignoring them. Or we may speak ill of them to others. Alas, the possibilities are nearly endless.

Of course one should never condone, much less encourage, harmful behavior. Harmful behavior must be brought to a halt if possible. In fact, this is precisely the point being made here: not to increase the harm. For this to be possible, each of us must come to understand our own motivations and impulses before adopting any course of action. The mind is all too easily deceived by anger, revenge, and self-justification, minimizing its own faults and even projecting them on others. It becomes small and narrow—bent on revenge, we lose sight of a wider range of compassionate and wise solutions. This narrowing is the activity of the kilesas and should be recognized as such. It is a mistake to adopt the kilesas as our framework. We should not cuddle them to our breasts, feed them, and allow them to fatten on our tenderness. Rather, dread, shame, fear, and abhorrence are the proper stance toward these forces in the mind. There is no need to feel sorry for hate. There is no need to indulge in greed. There is no reason to sweep ignorance under the rug—ignorance is not bliss.

If you can recognize your own destructive impulses, they will provide you with a wonderful opportunity to test the Buddha's instructions by putting yourself in the other person's place first. Make a careful inquiry. Whatever you are planning for that person, could you take it? Would you wish to endure that action yourself? If not, your plan is unjustified, an insult, and a transgression. Your own wild behavior will inflame your mind further, destroy the environment, and possibly harm others as well. It's not worth it—ever.

A timid attitude is appropriate when it comes to unleashing inner unwholesomeness.

Clearly, everything is better when cool heads and wholesome dhammas prevail.

## Benefits of Dhamma Vinaya

An unjust ruler is harsh and oppressive. He or she is unfair and brings the downfall of beings. Dhamma Vinaya is totally the opposite—an infallible way of raising one's standard of living. Based on reason, fully in accord with truth, Dhamma Vinaya uplifts one's thoughts and actions. It purifies, cultivates, refines, heals, and beautifies.

*Dhamma* means "that which carries, supports, uplifts, and saves." It is a set of guidelines for happiness. Vinaya consists of rules for refining one's behavior.

One who practices both Dhamma and Vinaya will grow skilled at dispelling all levels of defilement, from coarse and rude actions to the most subtle distortions of mind.

The word *kilesa,* "defilement," can also be translated as affliction, disturbance, torment of mind. The principal kilesas are ignorance, greed, and hatred. These forces are cruel and unfair rulers. When they get control they drag people down into suffering. Dhamma Vinaya is nothing other than a set of methods proven effective against these dreadful internal forces.

Mental defilements afflict the vast majority of beings and are at the root of almost all of humanity's collective problems. But does the Dhamma uplift every single person? Can Vinaya discipline stop everyone from being coarse and wild? Alas, obviously not. Nothing happens for beings who don't put these guidelines into practice. Each person must actually tread this path herself or himself.

To complete the Dhamma Vinaya four elements are needed. First, one learns the correct method of practice. Next, one undertakes the practice. Third, one gains the benefits. Finally one enjoys and applies those benefits. For example, when the Buddha suggests that we refrain from killing and points out the benefits, the first part of our training is hearing and understanding the instruction. For the second part, we refrain from violent, unjust deeds. By making this effort our internal enemies are cooled, and we are free from causing or incurring injury. We have gained the benefits. The result is that we find it easy to get along with others and they with us—we become easy to love, and enjoy a calm, fulfilling, happy state.

## Establishment in the Teachings

By refraining from wrongdoing, sīla sikkhā, we overcome transgressive kilesas, defined as those defilements which are strong enough to push us into shameful physical or verbal actions. As we further train our minds in concentration, samādhi sikkhā, we also gain control over the obsessive defilements, the torments of the mind. Finally, with paññā sikkhā, or insight wisdom, even latent defilements can be eradicated. Latent defilements include the deeply embedded unconscious and preconscious tendencies that cause us to react to unpleasant sensations with anger, to pleasant sensations with clinging, and to neutral sensations with ignorance, dullness, or distraction.

By overcoming successive layers of defilement we uncover deeper levels of peace within. Through moral actions, we stop agitating our external environment, and our life becomes more peaceful. With a cool, concentrated mind we experience a peace and happiness we never found before. As we train ourselves to be consistently mindful of body, speech, and mind, we are automatically developing good habits. Others may even take us as a role model.

Step by step, the benefits increase. This is called "being carried by the Dhamma." Our lives become simple and harmonious. With the arising of special insight we may ourselves become a natural expression of the teachings.

## Downfall

On the other hand, when basic morality is lacking we have fallen outside the Buddha's teachings. If we say we are Buddhist, it is only in name. Concentration and wisdom can't grow without the support of morality. Without all three trainings, we can't be freed from the bondage of defilements.

Deliverance, *vimutti,* is the goal and the purpose of Dhamma Vinaya. It is also an integral part of the training at all levels. If we practice restraint by, for example, suppressing a rude retort, at that moment we are freed from a transgressive defilement. If we practice concentration and turn the mind away from its obsessions, we free ourselves from obsessive defilements and also temporarily suppress the latent ones. When we reach nibbāna we will begin uprooting the latent defilements.

On the other hand, if we do not practice, we no longer remember the meaning of *vimutti*—a meaning that is not confined to a word, but is the experience of being freed from inner torment and thus, as a result, from the torment of one's own difficult, even addictive behavior patterns which are driven by unbearable mental states. If you think this description is excessive perhaps you have not observed yourself closely enough. If you watch yourself through any given day, observing the arising of desire and dislike, the sequence, say, of distraction, impatience, fantasy, dismay, and self-judgment, you will begin to understand that the ordinary mind is caught up in a rapid-fire sequence of mental states a large proportion of which is truly difficult to endure, and drives you to take whatever actions you believe will bring relief. We take this situation for granted, but when the possibility of vimutti, or inner freedom, can be borne in on us, we will understand completely why inner freedom is considered the most beautiful of all mental states.

Letting transgressive, obsessive, or subtle defilements take control, and doing nothing to counteract them, is called *papatita,* "downfall" or falling away. One is no longer carried, uplifted, and protected by

Dhamma Vinaya. One loses one's chance to reach greater levels of freedom.

The Buddha spoke of this in the Papatita Sutta, the Discourse on Downfall, part of the Aṅguttara Nikāya collection of discourses. The title word, *papatita,* is composed of *pa,* a particle that intensifies; and *patita,* meaning "to tumble, fall, or slip." The fall of papatita is therefore severe, disastrous. If we don't practice, our downfall will be catastrophic. What we fall into is suffering, for others as well as ourselves.

By taking refuge in the Buddha, listening to the teachings, and then applying them personally, we live according to a higher standard. But a committed, continuous effort is necessary, since as long as one remains an ordinary worldling, an unliberated *puthujjana,* one is bound to fall away from Dhamma Vinaya again and again. When this happens, one can only pick oneself up and keep trying.

On reaching the final path and fruition knowledge of arahantship, one receives full protection and safety. Liberation is the intent of Dhamma Vinaya, so please don't think of it as impossible. Make your best effort, and practice as much as you can. If you do not attain arahantship, you may at least taste one of the three lesser degrees of liberation along the way, becoming a *sotāpanna,* "stream-enterer"; a *sakadāgāmī,* "once-returner"; or an *anāgāmī,* "nonreturner." At each level, certain defilements are uprooted permanently, never to torture you again. With stream entry, all of the defilements lose some of their power, and one becomes immune not only from the worst behavior patterns, but also from the assumption that one's ego-self, or "I," is the true basis of one's being. In reality we are hoodwinked by this ego-belief, which tricks us into storing up an excessive amount of suffering.

## The Four Guardian Meditations

*Introductory Practices: The Four Guardian Meditations*

The ancient masters often began a period of training by establishing four protective meditations, known as *caturārakkhā-bhāvanā,* "four guardian meditations." *Bhāvanā* means "meditation" or "cultivation"; *catu,* "four"; and *ārakkhā,* "protection." The four have been practiced for more than two thousand years, and they are as effective for people today as they were for the ancient masters.

These four meditations can be practiced individually or as a group. They support and uplift the mind, develop happiness, and generally protect us from inner and outer dangers. Their protective quality is of chief importance; hence their title. During a satipaṭṭhāna vipassanā retreat in which we practice intensively, a few minutes per day is sufficient; they can also be undertaken in ordinary life in the form of brief recollections, or as part of one's daily sitting meditation practice. Some people develop practice of one or more guardian meditations extensively.

Protection and security are needed everywhere, especially in meditation practice. Many kinds of dangers can arise, inside the mind and outside it. External dangers are easy to identify. In Buddhist thought, they are called "distant" because they arise from outside one's own body and mind. These distant dangers are *puggalā vera,* "enemies of humanity" or "the enemy that comes in human form." We also face internal dangers, arising from within. In Pāḷi these are known as *kilesa vera* or *akusala vera,* "the enemy of mental defilements" and "the enemy of unwholesomeness."

Mental disturbance and unwholesomeness are dangerous enemies indeed. They live within us, as close as anything can be. Often, we even *claim* them as being an integral part of ourselves, not seeing that they are merely impersonal forces arising within the mind. Greed, hatred, and ignorance are the basic three kilesas, but they take myriad forms. One list of defilements from the suttas includes sixteen defilements: covetous or unrighteous greed, which we might understand as excessive selfishness that can lead to stealing, lying, or violent acquisition; ill will, anger, malice, contempt, domineering presumption, envy, jealous selfishness, hypocrisy and deceit, fraudulence, obstinacy, rivalrousness, conceitedness, arrogance or haughtiness, vanity, and heedless inconsideration—a callous lack of regard for others' welfare. Surely even without resorting to the texts, by now we have a sense of the kinds of forces in the psyche that destabilize us and destroy our happiness.

Obviously we need protection from both outer and inner enemies, but of the two, the inner enemy should be more terrifying. Nearly all of our outer problems are in fact caused by the inner enemies. Yet it is very rare to find genuine protection against the unwholesome, ugly, and divisive forces of the mind, however desperately we need it.

If we can stop the inner enemy from attacking us, we gain a special form of security called *gutti*. *Gutti* means being free from disturbances based in the activities of greed and hatred. Freed from the attacks of the inner enemy, we gain peace. Peace, when well established, is the basis for genuine happiness.

The four guardian meditations offer a certain level of prevention and protection; but only satipaṭṭhāna vipassanā meditation can permanently delete all of the defilements. Direct insight, rather than reflection, is the only method that can accomplish this. Therefore, even though you should practice the guardian meditations and enjoy them, you should keep in mind the possibility of ultimate safety and protection.

The first guardian meditation is *buddhānussati,* "recollecting the virtues of the Buddha." This is a very uplifting and inspiring practice; it consists of recognizing and reflecting on the Buddha and his virtues. The second guardian meditation is *mettā bhāvanā,* or loving-kindness meditation in which one wishes for the welfare and prosperity of others. The third is *asubha bhāvanā,* "contemplation of the impurity or foulness of parts of the body." The fourth is *maraṇasati,* "contemplation of death"—specifically, the developing of a sharp awareness that death can arise at any time.

# 2 *The First Guardian Meditation: Buddhānussati*

The essence of buddhānussati is to recognize that the Buddha is an enlightened one. This should be done frequently. To perform this meditation we may contemplate the Buddha himself or we may consider his virtues.

It is said the Buddha has infinite virtues. Buddhānussati meditation calls for thinking of them systematically, one by one. Let us consider his complete purity, *arahanta.*

The Buddha was completely lacking in the defilements of *rāga,* "greed" or "lust"; *dosa,* "anger"; and *moha,* "delusion." He was not polluted by these forces in any way. Generally, a buddha is one who is not burning up with mental defilements, who is unstained, fully purified. That is why a buddha is worthy of veneration.

The Buddha was an extraordinary being. Total purity may be hard to imagine, but with buddhānussati we begin to sense what it would mean to reach total purification from lust, hatred, and ignorance or delusion. The two basic forms of ignorance will be described in greater detail, but they can be thought of as limitation and distortion.

Purity was not some secret quality known only to the Buddha. In fact, his purity was so strong that it could not be hidden from others. It was palpable and obvious, manifesting as complete purity of mind, purity of speech, and purity of physical action.

Seeing him, people felt a natural awe and appreciation. The Buddha never sought approval nor expected others to make obeisance to him. It was part of his purity that he was not interested in making people into his students, other than for the purpose of showing them how to become genuinely happy and free. He gained a great following in his own time, and his teaching has survived until now, all because of his mental purification.

To the degree that we develop our meditation, we develop the Buddha's virtues. A person who meditates and practices Dhamma Vinaya as taught by the Buddha will gain the same purity to some extent. This is the only purpose of his teaching. In offering it, his motivation was pure, unerring, unselfish. As we begin to get a sense of his complete mental freedom and clarity, it helps us to trust the Buddha's instructions. A person who practices buddhānussati tends to feel more faith, respect, and confidence toward Buddhist teaching and culture. This faith becomes fuel for meditation practice.

If a meditator goes on to practice satipaṭṭhāna vipassanā meditation and thereby attains the first of the four path and fruition knowledges, that of stream entry, his or her faith will become unshakable. Path and fruition knowledge means tasting nibbāna, which is itself total purity and freedom from defilements. After that experience, one naturally recognizes this virtue. One realizes that one has practiced just as the Buddha practiced, and that one has felt the same kind of purity the Buddha felt, even though the degree of purification is lesser. Nonetheless, by tasting nibbāna one comes to the understanding that the Buddha's Dhamma is really true. This understanding, gained by oneself, can never be taken away.

As faith increases, one will never want to weaken the Buddha's teaching in any way. Instead one will want to develop and sustain the Buddha's teaching as much as one can. This desire for development is the most essential benefit of buddhānussati. One will sustain the teachings within one's self, and one will also try to support the teachings outwardly.

## Dhammānussati

Buddhānussati requires us to contemplate the virtues of a particular individual, namely, the historical Buddha. Some people prefer not to do this, and that is fine. They can instead contemplate the virtues of the Dhamma, a practice called *dhammānussati.* To develop this practice, one contemplates the virtue of the Dhamma, deeply and frequently.

One may choose to consider the Dhamma's uplifting qualities. The Dhamma never leads to the downfall of meditators or of any other beings, human or nonhuman.

There's a saying that the Dhamma is good in the beginning, good in the middle, and good in the end. Dhamma is good in the beginning in the sense that even by hearing just a little about the Dhamma, many people gain some peace of mind. Dhamma is good in the middle in the sense that during meditation practice one gains *samatha-sukha* and *vipassanā-sukha,* the happiness of tranquility and the happiness of insight. Dhamma is good in the end because it leads to the eradication of mental defilements, the attainment of total peace.

## Vision and Compassion

The Buddha's virtues are numerous. To discuss all of them in depth would make it impossible ever to practice satipaṭṭhāna vipassanā meditation! During a vipassanā retreat, moreover, just one or two minutes of buddhānussati per day suffice to fulfill its protective function. Still, it's good to say more about the Buddha's virtues, to give a sense of the vision and compassion on which Dhamma Vinaya is based and to provide a foundation for the daily recollection.

To begin with, all of the Buddha's qualities are perfect. He was flawless, completely satisfactory in every way. One virtue that may be especially interesting is *vijjā-caraṇa.* This term couples complementary virtues. *Vijjā* translates as "vision" or "knowledge." Closely related to wisdom, which is *paññā,* vijjā refers to special forms of knowledge that arise from Dhamma practice. As for *caraṇa,* it means basic teaching or basic conduct. It is a lovely contemplation to consider that the Buddha's compassion, his activity, and his teaching are all one, subsumed within a single word.

The texts describe fifteen kinds of caraṇa, all of which boil down to compassion, *karuṇā*. When working for the benefit of others, wisdom and compassion must both be present.

## *Memory, Clairvoyance, and Pure Vision*

Classically, *vijjā* is discussed in three or eight categories. Under the three-part system, the first type of special knowledge is *pubbe-nivāsa-anussati,* the ability to recollect past existences. This includes being able to see what kinds of existence one has taken before: a human, an animal, a hell being, an inhabitant of the celestial realms, and so on. It also includes recalling the details of what happened in those existences. As we all have had an infinite number of previous existences, each one filled with infinite details, this form of knowledge is quite vast.

The second special knowledge is *dibba-cakkhu-ñāṇa,* or clairvoyance, "divine-eye knowledge." The Buddha could see distant objects and events far beyond the capacity of the ordinary physical eye. It is said that *deva,* or celestial beings, also possess this form of vision; but the Buddha's *dibba cakkhu* was far better than the clairvoyance of a celestial being.

The third special knowledge is pure vision, *āsavakkhaya-ñāṇa,* which literally means "knowledge after the extinction of the biases," or undefiled knowledge. Everything human beings perceive through their sense doors is filtered through mental defilements. A human's ordinary state is to live in a fog of attachment, always desiring one thing or another and wallowing in the swamp of craving for future existence.

Though craving is quite palpable and pervasive, the most basic defilement is *avijjā,* "ignorance." Ordinary human beings are thoroughly drenched in its two forms. There is the ignorance of simple unknowing—our limited, incomplete, superficial knowledge of the world. On top of that, people also suffer from the ignorance of perverted knowing; our understanding is consistently distorted, mistaken, and contrary to the nature of reality. Both of these forms of ignorance are with us all the time.

But with pure vision *(āsavakkhaya-ñāṇa),* the moisture of the mental defilements dries up completely. Vijjā alone remains, and its fullest implication is omniscience. By totally dispelling both forms of ignorance, the Buddha came to know everything that can be known. When avijjā gives way to vijjā, understanding and knowledge are complete. A mind devoid of ignorance is the mind of a buddha, clear and limitless.

### *The Buddha's Compassionate Conduct*

Upon the Buddha's enlightenment, he had fully achieved his own awakening. Thereafter he dedicated his conduct to the benefit of others. His teaching is summed up in a single word, *caraṇa,* or conduct. As mentioned above, there are fifteen areas of caraṇa. These include *sīla,* "morality"; *suta,* "learning"; and *jhana,* "meditative absorptions," both mundane and transcendent. The fifteen areas of conduct boil down to one essential thing: karuṇā, or compassion.

Though the Buddha no longer suffered, he understood the suffering of others with omniscient empathy. Whenever he came into contact with the suffering of another being, he felt compassion and wanted that one's suffering to end, just as strongly as he himself had once wished to be free of his own suffering. He made no distinctions between himself and others in this respect. He realized, too, that beings have no secure refuge. That is why he taught Dhamma Vinaya indefatigably from shortly after his enlightenment until the very moment of his death.

Wisdom let him see what is beneficial and what is harmful, what leads to the happiness of beings and what brings suffering. Compassion made him act upon this knowledge. He constantly encouraged beings to adopt what is beneficial and reject what is harmful. Due to vijjā his advice was meaningful.

There is no better method than his teaching. Had the Buddha been able to enlighten others instantly, without asking them to make a personal effort, there would no longer have been suffering in the world.

### *Distinguishing Benefit and Harm*

As a buddha, one cannot be lacking in any aspect of vijjā-caraṇa, knowledge and conduct. If one's compassion is deficient, one will not help beings. Lacking wisdom, one is likely to give wrong or superficial advice. With wisdom and compassion both complete, a buddha's virtue is completely satisfactory.

The historical Buddha gained vijjā-caraṇa by encountering the dhamma, the truth about existence—which became the Dhamma or the doctrine that he taught. Encountering—or realizing—Dhamma also was the source of his omniscient vision. An incisive way to understand the nature of the Buddha's wisdom is to focus on his capacity to discriminate between benefit and harm. His discrimination was omniscient: he could see what was good not only for this life but also for future existences, not only for himself but for all beings. To distinguish benefit and harm accurately is equivalent to the term Dhamma.

Seeing the Dhamma, he recognized all possible forms of wrongful conduct along with their future consequences. Misconduct can be performed through the body, *kāya duccarita,* through speech, *vacī-duccarita,* or through the mind, *mano duccarita;* each form inevitably causes suffering. The Buddha did not want beings to encounter danger from their own unskillful behavior. Out of compassion, he put forth the Vinaya rules to counteract unskillful actions of body, speech, and mind. Though the discipline may seem difficult to follow at times, the Buddha's teaching never leads to torment. The Vinaya is an expression of compassion based on omniscient wisdom, a reliable guide for a life of happiness and ease.

Combining Dhamma wisdom and the compassion of the Vinaya, we have come full circle, re-encountering the Buddha's vijjā-caraṇa.

### *Saving Oneself, Saving Others*

The benefits arising from vijjā-caraṇa are incalculable. With āsavakkhaya-ñāṇa, or pure vision, the Buddha cut off his mental defilements forever. There was no more suffering for himself. With omniscient knowledge, *sabbaññutā-ñāṇa,* he saw how to extricate himself from the great predicament. Yet he didn't gain knowledge of deliverance and then gloat over it selfishly. With *mahā karuṇā,* "great compassion," he took the trouble to show others the escape route.

Had he not first saved himself, however, he could not have saved anyone else. This is a point we should keep in mind.

The Buddha's efforts to perfect himself began long, long before our own historical period. Eons ago, in a previous world system, he had an existence as a meditating hermit named Sumedha. Sumedha knew he was not free of suffering and that his own practice was incomplete. He also knew others were not free. Seeing clearly in this manner, he resolved to do whatever was necessary to save himself as well as others; this is called *mutto-moceyyaṃ.* This strong determination transformed him from an ordinary human being into a *bodhisattā,* a future buddha.

To live in *saṃsāra,* the cycle of existence, birth, and death, means that one cannot avoid old age, ill health, and death. Aging, decay, and death occur not just at the end of life, but second by second. In other words, one lives with much suffering. Only by the transformation known as "crossing the ocean of existence" can one be freed from it. Sumedha understood this, and he was determined to develop whatever special qualities he needed, not only to cross over to the other shore himself but to help others cross.

To reflect on Sumedha's determination is gratifying. It brings a realization of the magnitude of his endeavor, the courage needed to take on such a task.

The discourse known as the Cūlasaccaka Sutta uses the following expression about the Buddha: *Tiṇṇo so bhagavā taraṇāya dhammaṃ deseti.* This phrase means: "The Buddha, having crossed the ocean of suffering, taught Dhamma to others." The phrase is deliberately constructed so that the sequence of events is emphasized—first he saved himself, then he helped others. During his lifetime as Sumedha, although he had great courage, compassion, and a burning desire for liberation, he also had enough wisdom to recognize his present inability to help others, and enough compassion to want to be able to do it in the future. Though it must have seemed an inconceivably difficult, distant goal, he began his effort right there and then.

Teaching Dhamma with mere courage is not sufficient. It is important to teach Dhamma with compassion and profound knowledge.

In fact, teachers need to unite quite a few different qualities. Whether male or female, they must be worthy of respect, and lovable—qualities based on their personal ethical standards. They must also be willing to point out others' mistakes and to accept criticism of themselves. They must be profound in speech, able to discuss deep Dhamma subjects. And they must never abuse their disciples or urge them to needless, unreasonable efforts. All of these characteristics have many implications upon which we will not elaborate further here.*

Some people hold the view that saving others is more important than liberating oneself. They may even think the task of saving and helping others is so urgent that one's own liberation should be postponed. For these people, it may seem that saving oneself is a selfish activity, not truly or directly beneficial to anyone else. Since they feel the priority should be given to saving others, they may belittle practitioners who are trying to liberate themselves first.

Some years back, this question came up when I was conversing with a teacher from another religious tradition. I asked this teacher which was more important, saving oneself or saving others. The answer was that both were equally important, both should be practiced. I felt this was a fair answer, but I asked this teacher, "If you were stuck in mud up to your neck, and I too were stuck in mud up to my neck, would it be possible for me to pull you out?" The teacher replied that it would not be possible. Then, I countered, only when a person reaches dry land does he or she become capable of rescuing another. The Buddha himself taught along these same lines.

Having fulfilled vision and knowledge, *vijjā,* the Buddha was

*derived from Aṅguttara Nikāya VII, 34

able to liberate himself. Having fulfilled teaching, his compassionate conduct or compassion, *caraṇa,* he was able to save others. Mere compassion does not confer the ability to save anyone at all. Mere compassion cannot distinguish benefit from harm. On the other hand, mere vision and knowledge also leave one unable to liberate others. With mere vision and knowledge one lacks interest, doesn't care, and won't bother to save others. Great compassion is necessary to save others. This too is an important point.

Compassion caused the Buddha to teach whatever was necessary. Wisdom made him unafraid of the consequences of doing so.

The relationship of wisdom and great compassion is gratifying to reflect upon, and also to develop in oneself. Together they protect oneself and others. In the Buddha's case, being endowed with wisdom, or paññā, he no longer indulged in any wrongdoing of body, speech, or mind. Thus he no longer did anything harmful toward himself, but because of this, others didn't inherit any trouble from his actions either. Furthermore, he could see all the ways in which one's own misconduct brings pain and suffering to others. Because of this, compassion became an additional motivation for his perfect virtue.

## *Reciprocity of Wisdom and Compassion*

Let us examine this reciprocity more carefully, taking the first precept as an example. In Pāḷi it is *Pāṇātipātā veramaṇi sikkhāpadaṃ, samādiyāmi,* meaning "I will take great care to turn away and refrain from tormenting, killing, and torturing others."

In taking to heart this precept, one feels that any form of tormenting, ill-treating, or killing other beings is intrinsically disgusting and frightening. This is the wisdom aspect of morality. One vows to control one's behavior out of a sense of hiri and ottappa, that is, moral shame and fear of wrongdoing. Others are protected, too, but somewhat indirectly.

At the same time, this precept implies the equivalency of oneself and others. Just as one would not wish to be harmed, tormented, and murdered, one recognizes that others would not wish to endure these things. Now, self-control arises out of caring and consideration for others. This is the compassionate aspect of morality; it protects oneself, albeit indirectly. The full process works powerfully in both directions.

## Full Moon: What Is a Buddha?

We revere the Buddha because of his extraordinary qualities. But what, exactly, *is* a buddha? If you have read widely in the Buddhist literature, you may already have a good sense of the meaning of this term. Still, you may delight in reviewing the topic, and perhaps even find something new that will deepen your appreciation of this teaching, which will in turn support your practice of Dhamma Vinaya.

"Buddha" is not a given name. Rather it is a title given to any fully enlightened being. The historical Buddha of our era was born a prince named Siddhattha, born about more than 2,500 years ago in what is now southern Nepal. But there have been, and will be, countless other buddhas arising in the universe. Full enlightenment, buddhahood, means being totally liberated from suffering and also possessing the perfected qualities of a teacher. These include a compassionate motivation and extraordinary forms of knowledge, some of which were seen in the previous chapter.

### *Knowledge of the Four Noble Truths*

Most essentially a buddha is one who knows the Four Noble Truths about existence and instructs others about them, but there is more to it.

The Four Noble Truths encompass the definition of suffering, its cause, and its cure. These truths are valid at all times and in all situations. There are no Buddhist teachings that are not included in them. If a buddha knows all Four Noble Truths, then he knows all possible Buddhist teachings. Furthermore, a buddha possesses special forms of vision and understanding, including omniscience. Putting these two together, a buddha knows all *dhammas:* all knowable things, including all teachings.

A person may come to know the Four Noble Truths for herself or himself. This is wonderful, but it doesn't yet qualify that person as a buddha. Only one who knows the Four Noble Truths *perfectly*, and additionally desires to share them with all beings, can rightly be called a buddha.

Knowledge of the Four Noble Truths is not the mere ability to recite them in order, of course. We are speaking of an experiential understanding, a profoundly liberating gnosis.

One who has this genuine knowledge of the Four Noble Truths is called an *ariyā*, a noble one. The first stage or degree of liberation, reached by the sotāpanna or stream-enterer, takes place the first time the mind lets go of conditioned objects and enters into nibbāna, knowledge of cessation. At that moment certain fetters of mind are uprooted, discarded forever. Stream entry cuts off the wrong view of self and all the gross defilements that lead to rebirth in "states of loss," in conditions so difficult that freedom and even ease of mind are virtually unreachable. With continuing practice, insight knowledge deepens, and a noble stream-enterer can go on to become a noble once-returner, a nonreturner, or an arahant. Each stage loosens and breaks particular fetters of mind. Anger, craving, and ignorance are deleted one by one. Arahantship brings full liberation of the mind from the suffering of the kilesas.

There are also the *paccekabuddhas*, "silent buddhas," who are enlightened but do not teach the truth to the world. The fact that paccekkabuddhas do not teach is the reason why they are called silent.

## *Omniscience*

All of these noble and holy beings understand the truth to a profound degree, but they are not yet buddhas. For some, their knowledge is limited to the Four Noble Truths. They know the truth of suffering, the truth of the cause of suffering, the truth of freedom from suffering, and the truth of the path that leads to freedom from suffering. Others may come to know the Four Noble Truths along with other special knowledges such as *paṭisambhidā ñāṇa*, "knowledge of discernment," which grants fluency in giving discourses as well as insight into past causes and future results of particular events. Still, only a buddha knows the Four Noble Truths in association with all other related truths. A buddha simply knows everything that can be known. There is nothing beyond buddhahood; it is the supreme attainment.

The historical Buddha's life is recorded in the texts. We know a great deal about him, but most important is the fact that he reached buddhahood by practicing hard and gradually progressing in his meditation, just as any one of us would have to do. In terms of his buddhahood it's also important that in a previous existence he vowed to develop his *pāramīs,* or perfections, over the course of many lifetimes. After being born in our world, the Buddha reached the highest level of liberation, the path and fruition of holiness, *arahatta magga phala.* Together with this he attained omniscient knowledge, sabbaññutā-ñāṇa, plus other forms of extraordinary knowledge and vision as a result of his practicing the pāramīs. The title "Buddha" is reserved for one who knows all teachings and all things to be known. It is worth mentioning too that great compassion was the motivation for his attainment of this state.

### *How the Buddha Became a Buddha*

In our world a person who possesses much wealth and property is known as a millionaire. In parts of Asia, a person endowed with great education and knowledge will be called a "paṇḍita" (English uses the Indian form of this word, *pundit*). In the West, they may be a "doctor," "lawyer," "professor," or simply an "expert." Worldly titles like these may be chosen by oneself or granted by others. Sometimes an examination grants the right to use them.

It's different in the case of a buddha. Due to the power and momentum of his purity, the Buddha gained the path and fruition of arahantship along with omniscience and other outstanding forms of knowledge. In recognition of this great awakening, people simply began to call him the Awakened One, or the Buddha.

"Buddha" literally means "awakened one." This title was not bestowed by his parents, celestial beings, nor any other authority. It was a simple description of his perfected qualities.

### *Vesak*

May is the month called Vesak on the Buddhist calendar. The full moon of Vesak is celebrated throughout the Buddhist world. Often called "Buddha Day," it is the Buddha's birthday, the day he was born into this world as Prince Siddhattha. Much later, his enlightenment, *bodhi-ñāṇa,* took place on the full moon of Vesak; and on this day, too, his life also ended and he entered the great passing away, *mahāparinibbāna.*

Eons ago, it was also on this full moon day that the hermit Sumedha took a vow to free himself and all other beings from suffering, and on the same day the previous Buddha, Dipankara, confirmed that he, Sumedha, would succeed—that another Buddha would arise. It is quite an outstanding set of coincidences! We can add a minor event to the list, which is interesting although not emphasized in the texts. Some time after the Buddha attained enlightenment, his father, King Suddhodhana, invited him to visit. The Buddha accepted, and he reached Kapilavastu, his parents' home, on the full moon day of Vesak, Buddha Day.

All over the world Buddhists congregate on this day and reflect upon the Buddha's virtues.

### *The Buddha's Spiritual Biography*

Sumedha became a bodhisattā, a buddha-to-be, upon taking the vow to become fully enlightened. From that day forward he practiced the so-called three *cariyā,* three practices of a bodhisattā. These are *lokatthacariyā,* working for the benefit of the world; *ñātatthacariyā,* working for the benefit of relatives and fellow citizens; and *buddhattha-cariyā,* working toward becoming a buddha. Buddhattha-cariyā means developing the pāramīs as well as the actual attainment of buddhahood. The three cariyās lasted from his bodhisattā vow up to his attainment of enlightenment. After enlightenment, buddhattha-cariyā was no longer needed, since his buddhahood was complete. He worked entirely for the benefit of others and the world.

We could say there are five chapters in the Buddha's spiritual biography. His story begins on the day when Sumedha takes the vow which sets him on his course. As a bodhisattā, he practices the three cariyās for many thousands of lifetimes. This long time span is the main body of the first chapter.

The second chapter opens with his birth into our world as Prince Siddhattha. As the prince grows up, he maintains the three cariyās.

The third chapter begins when he abandons royal life. Siddhattha becomes an ascetic, undertaking six years of arduous spiritual searching, still with the goal of becoming a buddha. At the end of this chapter, he recognizes the futility of austerities and gives them up. He realizes the need to observe his actual experience moment by moment: that is, he discovers satipaṭṭhāna vipassanā meditation.

The fourth chapter starts when he completes the work required for becoming a buddha and attains enlightenment and omniscience under the Bodhi tree. This chapter spans the forty-five years during which he teaches and works for others. Throughout this time he still practices the first two cariyās, lokatthacariyā and ñātatthacariyā, working for the benefit of the world and his fellow citizens. He teaches with omniscient knowledge and great compassion, mahā karuṇā, as well as with *desanā-ñāṇa,* knowledge of teaching.

The fifth and final chapter in the Buddha's life is his final passing away. Upon his deathbed, he tells his disciples that Dhamma Vinaya will remain as their teacher after he is gone. He admonishes them to practice lokatthacariyā and ñātatthacariyā, but also to work hard for their own personal benefit by undertaking the three trainings of morality, concentration, and wisdom. If they want to vow to become buddhas themselves, he does not forbid it, nor does he require it. Disciples should seek their own liberation from suffering without forgetting the benefit of others. They should teach Dhamma Vinaya in addition to practicing it.

### *Inhuman Beings*

Beings face danger all the time; beings lack peace. This can be verified any day by reading the newspaper, listening to the radio, or watching TV.

The human population in the world has risen to the billions. There are many diverse groups and types of people, but all are vulnerable to the same problems and dangers. There is danger or fear of disease. There is danger or fear from *amanussa*—literally, inhuman beings—violent enemies in human form. Finally, there is the danger or fear of famine. Due to these three major fears, people suffer physically and mentally, and lack peace.

The worst danger comes from the amanussa. These are human beings who have lost, or never attained, full humanity. *Inhumane* partly describes what they are, but in fact they most often seem to resemble demons. The term *amanussa* refers to a person who lacks the most basic morality, sīla. Such a person's mind is uncultivated and not fully formed. Lacking knowledge and understanding, amanussa are unruly and subject to manipulation by distorted ideas.

Because of the existence of these beings and the disturbances they cause, leaders have arisen all over the world to tackle and control them, and to protect the rest of us from them. Leaders may feel they are working toward the liberation of beings from suffering; yet an overwhelming majority of leaders remains in the category of ordinary worldlings, meaning that they are still susceptible to being overwhelmed by the kilesas. They also continue to hold all kinds of wrong views, including the belief in an ultimately solid self, plus other partial and biased views.

Despite their limitations, such leaders often do work hard for the physical and mental happiness of others. They can feel a deeply positive volition, *cetanā,* as a basis for their work. Such a leader thinks, "I work for the benefit of others," but at the same time guards only the happiness of certain beings while attacking others. These leaders are also susceptible to pride and conceit, particularly of the sort known as *atimāna,* conceited haughtiness. Without being completely aware of what they are doing, these leaders begin to put atimāna to the fore. Instead of serving other beings, they serve rigid, selfish conceit and thereby, again, devolve into the status of the amanussa.

### *The True Refuge from Danger and Death*

Sumedha was horrified by the recognition that it was not just himself who suffered, but that all living beings must get old, become sick, and eventually die. There must be a solution to this, he thought. Though he could have escaped the situation all alone, he resolved to develop the capacity to save all beings.

Renouncing the happiness of nibbāna in that lifetime, he developed his virtue over an infinite number of existences. Not yet a buddha, he was merely a human being like ourselves. Thinking of Sumedha can inspire us when we encounter difficulties in practice. Compassion is what gave him the necessary courage and endurance.

Great compassion, mahā karuṇā, was the basis upon which the Buddha-to-be developed the perfections. When he finally attained omniscient knowledge and enlightenment knowledge, sabbaññutā-ñāṇa and bodhi-ñāṇa, he dried up all of the kilesas, the taints and cankers of the mind. During the following years he taught the Dhamma for the welfare and happiness of human and celestial beings. He was tireless in his effort to help. Out of twenty-four hours he usually rested only two to three, or four at most.

### *The Fairest of Systems*

The Buddha's Dhamma Vinaya is different from ordinary thought systems and political systems like communism, socialism, capitalism, and other philosophies. These were invented by worldlings, puthujjanas steeped in mental defilements. They are flawed, therefore, and tainted by greed, hatred, and delusion. On the other hand, the Buddha's Dhamma is quite impartial and unbiased. It is balanced, egalitarian, and totally compassionate. All who practice Dhamma Vinaya, whether they are human beings, celestial beings, or

Brahmas residing in worlds without physical substance, will receive benefits in precise accord with their efforts and abilities.

In the Buddha's doctrine there is no desire to gain the upper hand. Nor is there any part of the philosophy that encourages us to let others get the upper hand over us. Everyone who practices the teaching will gain benefit and happiness from it.

If you do choose to follow Dhamma Vinaya you are bound to experience it fully. Your behavior will become well-shaped and you are certain to receive all of the benefits, including freedom from suffering. This assumes, of course, that you make the necessary effort!

### *Gaining the Dhamma for Oneself*

It is beautiful and important to reflect on the Buddha and his virtues, but only by seeing the Dhamma can one truly and accurately see the Buddha for oneself. As the Buddha once said, "He or she who sees the Dhamma, sees me." True buddhānussati means traveling the path the Buddha also traveled. Only by practicing Dhamma Vinaya can one fulfill the intent of the Buddha's compassion.

To gain the benefits of Dhamma Vinaya, the texts offer the following four guidelines:

1. *Sappurisa-saṃseva:* associate with a person who is knowledgeable and can teach the Dhamma.
2. *Saddhamma savaṇa:* hear the correct teachings.
3. *Yoniso-mānasikāra:* engage wise attention. This means directing one's life wisely, as well as maintaining upright behavior in all circumstances.
4. *Dhammānudhamma paṭipatti:* practice well in accordance with Dhamma Vinaya.

These days many people are not well versed in Buddhist literature; they do not apply the teachings correctly. Such people will slip from the correct path. If you're careful to fulfill these four requirements, your contact with Dhamma Vinaya will be worthwhile. If you don't fulfill them, beware, for you could be wasting an amazing opportunity—a human life.

### *Importance of Retreats*

Meditation practice leads us to gain insight, the eye of wisdom that understands what the Buddha understood and what he was trying to teach. Attending intensive meditation retreats fosters maximum depth of practice and exposes you to the guidance of qualified teachers. Retreats, then, support the first, third, and fourth guidelines above.

On retreat, internal and external purity are easier to achieve than in everyday life. Both of these forms of purity are indispensable for anyone who wants to develop insight. External purity refers to external cleanliness: cleanliness of the body and the environment. A proper retreat environment should be simplified, clean, and tidy. One must also bathe and generally keep the body clean, outside and inside.

Silence is another benefit of meditation retreats. The most extreme form of purifying speech, silence is extraordinarily helpful in reducing the chaos and disturbance of the mind—which is the meaning of internal cleanliness. More deeply, however, it is through mindfulness, labeling and observing all arising objects, that internal purity arises.

We will deal with mental purification extensively in subsequent chapters of this book. Basically, however, it must be emphasized that continuous mindfulness is far easier to achieve in a retreat environment than in a busy, complex worldly life. If you are at all able to set aside time for a retreat, of course you must encourage yourself to choose that option, even if it means giving up something else, like a vacation. And once you have entered an intensive practice period, please, *please,* do not waste the opportunity in distraction and laziness. Retreat time is precious. You never know when, or whether, you can come back again!

If you practice deeply you may encounter the experience of nibbāna, genuine knowledge of Dhamma, and the Four Noble Truths. Meditation practice is the one and only way to gain and experience this. There is no other way. When nibbāna has been experienced, one is said to be fulfilled with wisdom, paññā. After that, a person will naturally wish for others to experience the same nibbānic peace, a happiness that is truly out of this world.

With one's own attainment of the Dhamma, one gains genuine loving-kindness, mettā, a wish that others will attain the same benefit. One will also feel karuṇā, compassion, for their suffering. A person who has attained the Dhamma will always tend to encourage their near and dear ones to practice. In this way they naturally fulfill the two forms of conduct—helping the world and helping other people, lokatthacariyā and ñātatthacariyā.

Try to venerate the Buddha in the highest way, through your own meditation practice.

# 3 *The Second Guardian Meditation: Mettā*

Loving-kindness, mettā, protects the mind from hatred and greed. It is practiced by a great many people throughout the Buddhist world. The word mettā translates simply as "friendly," also as "moist," or "sticky." This is the nature of loving-kindness. When it is present, there is friendliness and a sense of cohesion, sticking together.

Loving-kindness arises easily and naturally whenever the mind takes as its object a dear person, known as a *piyamanāpa-puggala;* or indeed when thinking of any person whose character is amiable and pleasant. Some wonderful aspect of a person can also be the object of loving-kindness. Later, by developing mettā bhāvanā in a concerted way, we can also take neutral or unpleasant people as objects of loving-kindness without diminishing our capacity to wish them well.

Analyzing it as a mental state, mettā is a form of *adosa cetasika,* a "mental factor of nonhatred." Mettā arises in the absence of hatred, *dosa,* and is, in fact, diametrically opposed to it. Dosa's nature is to destroy and break up. Mettā, as its opposite, builds support, cohesion, and welfare among sentient beings. Adosa is well intentioned, while dosa bears an ill-intentioned quality.

When perceiving a disagreeable person or a disagreeable aspect of a person, consciousness goes dry. In nature, any dry material breaks up easily. Dry skin cracks and doesn't function properly to protect the body. Hatred, when it is present, cracks and destroys the mind. Hatred is also said to burn up its own support. It burns the mind, burns the person, and brings harm and destruction to others. Dosa is indeed a very frightening thing.

Loving-kindness—juicy and cohesive—makes relationships feel agreeable and pleasant.

The winter season in northern climates damages the body. If there's no protection, the skin dries, the lips crack. Distress arises. Moisturizers, oils, and lip balm are needed to repair existing damage and prevent further problems. Then people can feel happy again. Similarly, though more severely, hatred damages, dries, and cracks the mind. Well-being vanishes. If, on the other hand, loving-kindness is strongly developed, one feels protected, happy, and good.

Mettā and dosa cannot really coexist. Therefore, cultivating one means banishing the other.

Human beings do not live by themselves. We all inhabit a social context, connected to family, friends, relatives, and associates. We also clump together in villages, towns, cities, districts, and nations. Relating to one another in all of these contexts, we always need loving-kindness.

Two pieces of dry material won't stick together. Nor can glue create a strong bond if it is applied to just one side. Before they'll stick together, both elements need to be well smeared. If everyone applied loving-kindness in their relationships, families and societies would cohere harmoniously.

When people quarrel it brings dissatisfaction. Soon, if the quarrel is not resolved, those involved will separate; both will suffer. People who don't recognize the value of mettā find it easier to become dissatisfied with each other and more easily break apart. This should be blamed on one thing only, and that is the destructive nature of hatred, dosa, which causes disturbance to oneself and others, leads to dissatisfaction, and finally to separation or worse.

## Characteristic, Function, and Manifestation of Mettā

In the texts loving-kindness is defined by its characteristic, *lakkhaṇa;* its function, *rasa;* its manifestation, *paccupaṭṭhāna;* and its proximate cause, *padaṭṭhāna.* This fourfold definition should be understood.

The characteristic of mettā is to wish for the welfare and benefit of others. In Pāḷi this is *hitakāra-pavatti-lakkhaṇa,* a long word meaning that the presence of well-wishing in the mind is the *lakkhaṇa,* or characteristic sign, of mettā. One wishes others to be well, free from disease, happy, and successful in every possible way. With this lakkhaṇa present, one also feels satisfied in one's own mind. If dosa is there instead, that sense of satisfaction is unavailable.

Loving-kindness cannot just stay on a mental level. It has to manifest as sweet words and bodily actions governed by loving-kindness. This is the *rasa,* or function, of loving-kindness. In Pāḷi it is *hitūpasaṃhāra-rasa,* meaning that mental actions are complemented and strengthened by verbal and bodily actions, i.e., the act of goodwill toward others.

When mettā is expressed in action, it grows powerful—strong enough to drive away any grudge or resentment that may have existed. People who tend to carry grudges and resentments, whether toward other people or situations, end up with lots of problems in their lives. Free of grudges and resentments, one can lead a relatively peaceful, unproblematic existence. *Āghāta vinaya paccupaṭṭhāna,* "lack of grudges or the removal of ill will," is the manifestation of mettā.

Loving-kindness also works to pacify dosa. Hatred, the destroyer, is an inner enemy of the mind, arising from within as a form of akusala vera or kilesa vera, the enemy of unwholesomeness and the enemy of defilement. Hatred and mettā compete, just as the skin's natural oils and moisture compete against harsh winds. Sometimes, the skin's natural defenses are overwhelmed and need help from outside. In ordinary life, too, we need to train ourselves to increase our secretions of mettā-moisture, so it can protect us when hatred mounts and threatens to overwhelm the mind.

It's important to pinpoint the proximate cause for loving-kindness, meaning the quickest or most efficient way to cause mettā to arise. This is the capacity to see the lovable aspects of another person or group of people. These lovable aspects can take the form of kindness through bodily behavior, pleasant speech, or agreeable mental attitudes. We may notice the sweet, wonderful way another person has of continuously helping others, or of giving and sharing whatever they have. Maybe they are consistently virtuous, or refined and well behaved. The more skilled one becomes in detecting what is good, pleasant, and positive about others, the more loving-kindness will automatically arise.

It is equally important to train oneself to ignore the hateful aspects of another person or a group of persons and to emphasize their lovable side instead. This requires wise, directed attention. When wise attention, *yoniso-mānasikāra,* is present, one sees in a straightforward manner. When it is absent one tends to dwell on the negative, perceiving people and life in a lopsided and distorted way. To avoid poisoning one's life with negativity, it is crucial to learn how to discover, focus on, and stick with what is lovable and positive in ourselves and others.

If one cannot find any lovable aspects in oneself, in another person, or in a group, then hateful qualities will dominate one's perceptions. One will see nothing but flaws and difficulties everywhere. Dosa has taken over the mind, making it dry, stiff, tense, and difficult. As a result one's bodily behavior also becomes tense and difficult. In an untrained mind, dosa overpowers mettā all too often.

## *Selfish Love and Selfless Love*

Genuine loving-kindness, mettā, arises easily toward nice people and those who are already close to us. At the same time, however, *taṇhā,* or craving, and *pema,* or attachment to one's near and dear ones, are likely to come in as well. Selfish attachment often poses as mettā.

Since craving has a deceptive quality, we have to be on guard. Most people never learn the difference.

Love governed by selfishness, craving, and attachment to near and dear ones also feels moist and sticky. There is adherence, a sense of sticking to the object. Ordinary people think this is what is meant by loving-kindness, and they consider attached love to be a wholesome mental state. Real mettā is by nature pure and unattached. The loving-kindness of a holy arahant is said to be *kiriya,* a word which means "inoperative." Purity of mind alters the nature of love.

Love governed by *taṇhā-pema* has to be considered as somewhat unwholesome because it is tainted by self-centeredness. The love experienced among family members, between father and daughter, mother and son, husband and wife, and among other relatives is not one hundred percent genuine mettā, unfortunately.

Self-centered love is okay as long as things go according to our own wishes, beliefs, and desires. But when people stop behaving as we want them to, or something else comes up that's contrary to our preferences, we quickly run out of patience. We become unwilling to make sacrifices. Sooner or later we fly into a rage and even explode. True loving-kindness is not like this. Mettā has a quality of being unlimited. One wishes for the welfare and happiness of others—at all times. Even when being insulted by another person, one feels patience, forgiveness, and a willingness to sacrifice.

This is where karuṇā, compassion, comes in. Karuṇā is associated with mettā in a group of meditations called the *brahmavihāra,* or divine abodes. It gives us the strength and courage to face the issues that inevitably come up between us without selfishness, anger, and confusion. We stop contributing to the overall problem—unlike with taṇhā-pema, which usually leads to a confused and stressed-out state of mind.

The texts have another word for attached love—*gehasita-pema,* "love of one's own house or family." This is a love that is limited, circumscribed by craving and attachment. Ānanda, who was the Buddha's attendant for many years, felt tremendous love and attachment for the

Buddha. Because of gehasita-pema, as long as the Buddha was alive, Ānanda could not gain full insight into the Dhamma. Even though he was constantly in the presence of the world's supreme teacher, he remained a stream-enterer, unable to attain full liberation from all defilements. Only after the Buddha's demise was he able to cut off gehasita-pema and gain the Dhamma as an arhant.

### *Mettā within a Family*

At this point, the question may arise whether genuine mettā ever really does exist between husband and wife, parents and children, or other relatives. Well, yes, it does—albeit intermittently. In some families the arising of genuine loving-kindness is very frequent. The parents and the children are well intended toward one another, so there tends to be harmony and unity. Problems inevitably crop up, but since the family members can forgive each other, they resolve each situation as it comes along. They stay connected for a long time, only because genuine loving-kindness arises again and again among them. The texts illustrate the benefits of loving-kindness with the following parable.

Once upon a time there was a cow nursing her calf. During this process a hunter appeared and shot the calf with an arrow. To his dismay, the arrow bounced off without hurting the calf in any way. The calf had been protected by the love of the mother cow. As human beings we enjoy a higher status—our capacity for loving-kindness is of a higher order than a cow's, or at least it should be. We should strive to fulfill our true human potential in this sense. Mettā, especially if we have seen the need to develop it strongly, can become strong enough to deflect many kinds of troubles and travails.

Some people say they are so much in love with another person that they can't bear to be separated even for a few hours. Surely this type of intense attachment is unwholesome, akusala. If loving-kindness is stronger than self-centered interest, a person can bear some periods of separation, allowing loved ones a greater independence without any decrease of loving feeling.

### *Near and Distant Enemies*

*Taṇhā,* or craving, and *pema,* attachment to one's near and dear ones, is called the near enemy of mettā because attachment so often masquerades as genuine loving-kindness. Self-interest and mettā arise intermittently, appearing to be mixed together. Meanwhile hatred, dosa, is called the far or distant enemy because its nature is distinctly opposed. When hatred is present, loving-kindness is usually far away; and it's hard to mistake one for the other.

Normally if people work on developing loving-kindness, they are usually doing it for their own benefit. A husband and wife who live together generally want to relate to each other harmoniously; yet they are always keeping their own benefit in mind. This type of love qualifies as taṇhā-pema, a love that hopes for something in return. True mettā, loving-kindness, does not contain a desire for one's own benefit.

### *Benefiting Others, Benefiting Oneself*

When hate arises, loving-kindness is thoroughly blocked. Also, when selfish affection or lust slips into our minds, our judgment is clouded and our responses distorted. Without knowing it, we're really putting ourselves first. We have met again our old enemies, akusala vera and kilesa vera (the enemy of unwholesomeness and the enemy of defilement); hatred and lust are mental pollutants that fill us with torment and impurity. In contrast, a mind genuinely imbued with mettā is clear, filled instead with a sense of unrestricted friendliness. At that time the mental afflictions are far away.

To illustrate the concept of the near and distant enemies, let us think of a boxing match. Sometimes boxers take big swings, trying to strike with the greatest force. At other times they hit from close quarters at an unexpected moment. The haymaker punch is easy to see coming, easier for a boxer to avoid. But the sucker punch is hard to defend against—a boxer can get knocked out without knowing what hit him. Similarly it's much easier to avoid the big dosa-punch than the sneak attacks of taṇhā-pema or gehasita-pema. The limited forms of love pose as loving-kindness and can be very hard to assess properly. Because of the great potential for confusion, there's a need to educate oneself, to get clear, and recognize the nature of selfish love.

It is also good to research the value of loving-kindness for oneself. Practical experiments can be done at no cost. Try offering a smile to another person and you will probably get a smile in return. If you greet someone with sweet words, a sweet response is likely to come back. If you give directions to someone lost in town or help a fellow traveler with his or her luggage on a train or bus, you are likely to receive a heartfelt thank-you. You're also likely to think pleasant thoughts such as "I've done my civic duty." A sense of happiness and satisfaction will arise in you.

Dhamma can be understood as guidelines for happiness—the benefit and welfare of all sentient beings. As such, it can be practiced by anyone regardless of religious affiliation. You might say Dhamma is merely the best way of being human. Who refuses a helping hand? If the offer of help is truly based in the wish to bring happiness to another person or group, and there's no selfish motivation hidden behind it, then it is rare for the help to be rejected.

Mettā, loving-kindness, is essentially the desire to benefit others. It fulfills the aspect of Dhamma that is relational. The simple, fundamental principle of kindness can—and should—be practiced by every single person.

When we meet a being in a difficult situation, we will naturally try to help. This impulse springs naturally from mettā. Sooner or later, too, our kindness is likely to be returned. Somebody we've helped will offer us a kindness; or perhaps kindness will arrive from an unexpected quarter. Mettā is so badly needed in this world: it should be embraced by one and all as a basic human principle.

Remember: mettā is defined as wishing and working for the happiness and welfare of others. Even though it is good for oneself, notice that its definition contains not a single word about cultivating one's own benefit. Mettā must be free from all hints of self-centeredness.

We must never calculate, "So, if I help you, what's in it for me?" Yes, mettā is pleasant and satisfying in itself; it often bears fruit that is highly desirable. Still, real mettā is aimed purely at others' well-being.

Mettā is considered wholesome, kusala. When it's truly selfless, it touches the realm of the perfections, the pāramīs. Selfless loving-kindness is a step toward buddhahood.

## The Abodes

Mettā bhāvanā, loving-kindness meditation, is the second guardian meditation. It is also the first member of another group of practices known as the four brahmavihāras, limitless or divine abodes. These meditations are closely related to loving-kindness practice and can be said to extend, amplify, and complete it. Besides loving-kindness the brahmavihāras include compassion, *karuṇā;* sympathetic joy, *muditā;* and equanimity, *upekkhā.*

Any work that relieves others' suffering is called a noble practice. These brahmavihāras, then, are also called the four *brahmacariyā,* or noble practices. Though highly developed in meditation—within the mind—the development of loving-kindness, compassion, sympathetic joy, and equanimity is not meant to be restricted to the mental level alone. All of these noble practices must be developed verbally and expressed in physical actions, too. The word *bhāvanā* means meditation but also, more generally, development.

We have already mentioned many of the essential things to be known about loving-kindness. We have also said that everyone should practice it. Much of what we have said can be applied to the other brahmavihāras, about which we will now speak briefly.

### *Karuṇā Bhāvanā, Development of Compassion*

There are two kinds of *dukkhita,* or suffering beings. Some suffer from outer problems such as illness or destitution, disease, sorrow, or lack of refuge. Others are, or have been, involved in *duccarita,* "misconduct." They took a wrong path and therefore remain behind, in suffering. Compassion should be extended to both types of dukkhita.

Someone who's in a tight spot naturally wants help. Then, of course, it is most satisfying when help arrives. The situation is even better if help is accepted. We must never refuse to give or receive help, whether physical, verbal, or in the form of thoughts.

As with mettā, the Pāḷi texts offer a four-part definition of karuṇā: in terms of its characteristic or nature, its function, its manifestation, and its proximate cause. Compassion has the characteristic of wanting to remove others' suffering. We try to support suffering beings outwardly, if their difficulties come from outside; or we may offer counsel and try to set them straight in the case where their troubles are self-inflicted. In both cases we wish to benefit the other person, helping him or her to be free of suffering.

Compassion brings on a certain form of distress, *anukampā,* or suitable mental quivering or trembling. Anukampā is an inability to endure the knowledge that others are suffering; it is the function of compassion. There's an urge to do something constructive about the painful situation. Anukampā is not the same as ordinary sorrow, *soka,* a word often translated as "grief." Grief is another type of mental agitation that can arise in the face of others' suffering; but it is considered unconstructive and unsuitable.

Soka, grief, is caused by certain changes in the mind. When we first come into contact with suffering beings, as soon as we recognize their suffering we wish them to be freed of it. However, as time goes on this pure karuṇā often devolves into a subtle form of anger or aversion. This is what is meant by soka; as the texts explain, it poses as compassion. Coming across a suffering being again and again, one sooner or later begins wishing to resolve the case as quickly as possible. This may seem to be wholesome, genuine compassion, but in fact the mind has become unhappy and wants to turn away. One may feel afraid, tired, helpless; one wants to separate oneself from that being. This is not genuine compassion.

When a sense of distaste or even a destructive intent appears, setting oneself apart from the suffering being, it is a clue that this may not be time to take action. Unclear, distorted views are likely to be present; hatred has disguised itself as compassion, and we've been hoodwinked.

When wise people encounter suffering beings they usually experience anukampā, the suitable form of mental quivering or trembling. But even wise people's minds can get tainted with dislike. We all must watch carefully over our minds, lest destructive intentions trick us into making mistakes.

On festival days in one of India's states, Assam, the locals collect snails and throw them into boiling water. Snails need help, according to a folk belief, because they're so slow-moving. So let's bring them to a quick end in a cooking pot! Now the snails can be reborn in a nimbler form of existence.

The snail festival may sound weird, but we too may have been guilty of doing similar "favors" for others. People talk about "teaching him a lesson" or doing things "for your own good." Before we grant to ourselves the right to inflict unpleasant experiences on others, we might ask ourselves whether we would enjoy being on the receiving end. Any form of torment is cruel. We must always try to act with a constructive intention, within an undistorted vision of life.

There are many causes for the arising of compassion, but seeing the suffering of helpless beings is the proximate or most immediate. We will not turn away from suffering or try to blame those who are experiencing it. As soon as we understand the brute fact of their suffering, this recognition brings up a spontaneous compassion. If we want to develop compassion, we will make deliberate efforts to become more sensitive and understanding when faced with the pain of others. As our discernment grows, our desire to remove suffering increases and any callousness will disappear. We will be more and more reluctant to bring suffering to anyone. A mind without cruelty is the manifestation of karuṇā.

Like mettā bhāvanā, karuṇa bhavana approaches life in a basic, irrefutable manner. It should be easily understood by all people, regardless of particular beliefs. There is so much suffering in the world—it would be good if karuṇā bhāvanā were cultivated by everyone. This means compassionate action, compassionate speech, and a compassionate mind.

### *Muditā Bhāvanā, Development of Sympathetic Joy*

Sympathetic joy means rejoicing in the happiness of others without envy or the slightest wish to reduce their happiness. Muditā is a wonderful mental factor. We feel joy when seeing another person gain property or social status, succeed in their work or profession, win many friends or followers, and acquire a good reputation or fame. Truly, who would reject genuine sympathetic joy if it is offered? Clearly muditā is a practice that ought to be carried out by everyone!

As praiseworthy as muditā is, it is also fairly rare. Ordinarily when people see someone else endowed with great property and wealth they feel a little less than happy. In fact the normal reaction is jealousy and envy. Jealousy is the distant enemy of sympathetic joy, muditā. Muditā is constructive by nature whereas jealousy is rather destructive. They are opposed.

When mettā and karuṇā are strong, so is sympathetic joy. The brahmavihāras build upon each other. You see, the nature of mettā is friendliness—one feels satisfied with the other being. The presence of loving-kindness also means freedom from dosa, ill will; instead, there's an unselfish desire to support the welfare and happiness of others.

A person filled with mettā is also patient, able to forgive others' mistakes, and willing to make sacrifices for others' benefits. This shades naturally into a sense of compassion for other beings whenever they happen to be in pain. Compassion, karuṇā, involves both a deep sympathy for others and a lack of cruelty toward them. So a person who is kind and compassionate will feel real joy on meeting someone else who happens to be successful, wealthy, prosperous, fortunate. There will be no cruelty, no hidden wish to spoil that person's happiness.

Unselfishness is at the heart of mettā, karuṇā, and muditā. When loving-kindness and compassion are pure, one genuinely rejoices in the success of others. But if these feelings are not quite genuine, one only makes a pretense of being happy about another person's success. Inside, one feels envious, discomfited. Beware of deceitful, fake smiles and fake supportive speech posing as genuine muditā.

The characteristic of muditā is wishing to support another person's success. One is free from jealousy, that form of ill will which brings along a destructive intent in response to others' fulfillment. When muditā is present the mind is clear. A bright, clean, open mind is the manifestation of sympathetic joy. One feels great satisfaction within oneself—even if one's adversaries and opponents are victorious.

The proximate cause of muditā is the ability to recognize and rejoice in others' success. As muditā develops one will wish others to be fulfilled in every possible way, and it becomes gratifying to contemplate others' prosperity and property.

It is worth noting that muditā doesn't imply that one has to downgrade one's own enjoyment of status, property, and wealth. To see others enjoying high status is wonderful, and it is just as gratifying to contemplate one's own good fortune. To count the number of someone else's friends, followers, and disciples brings a profound joy—but so does contemplating one's own friends, followers, and disciples. Seeing others' virtues or one's own virtues, others' possessions or one's own possessions, equal satisfaction will arise.

On the other hand, without muditā, one finds the success of others unbearable. Jealousy pollutes the mind. Envious plans may arise, a form of *ayoniso-mānasikāra,* ill-directed attention. If this happens one must deliberately apply the proximate cause of muditā, and try to savor the satisfactions of other beings.

Everybody should support this kind of clarity and purity. Meanwhile, it's important not to accept fake sympathetic joy, those deceitful smirks and false compliments that really arise out of envy. When a person cannot be happy about another person's fulfillment or prosperity, false muditā will appear. False muditā is not based on a genuine wish to support the happiness of others.

If loving-kindness, compassion, and sympathetic joy have not yet arisen, one should make a strong effort to encourage them. When they have appeared, one should strengthen and develop them. If they occur only rarely one should practice so that they come up frequently.

### *Upekkhā Bhāvanā, Development of Equanimity*

When mettā is mixed with rāga, lust, one becomes more partial to certain beings than others. This mixed-up love poses as a wholesome mental state, as we have seen. Similarly, if there's some imbalance in one's concern for others, pure compassion eventually gets mixed up with sorrow and aversion. But when there's a true lack of bias, impartiality toward all beings, one is full of good wishes and yet remains free of worry. This is the state of upekkhā, or equanimity, the fourth and final noble practice.

The characteristic or nature of equanimity is a balanced view of sentient beings. Its function is an unbiased impartiality; and its manifestation is the state of mind in which there is neither ill will nor attached love. It is a state of perfect balance. Upekkhā is the Dhamma of neutrality; it is a wholesome mental state.

Equanimity has a variety of causes, but the proximate or most immediate is to understand that beings are experiencing the results of their own past actions, kamma. A person who is lucky and encounters good fortune has done many good things in the past, while someone who goes through a lot of problems has done unwholesome deeds. One should develop this kind of balanced, impartial view.

All human beings live in social groups. Whether we admit it or not, we all have obligations toward others. Whenever we enter into a group activity, we need loving-kindness, mettā. When someone is in trouble, we have to apply compassion, karuṇā. When somebody is successful and prosperous we should support them with sympathetic joy, muditā. There are times, however, when none of these attitudes is appropriate.

Furthermore, as we have seen, each noble practice has a tendency to veer off into an unwholesome state. Loving-kindness gets mixed up with self-centered desire, compassion with aversion and fear. Muditā freezes into faked sincerity.

We need to find a fulcrum—some wholesome mental factor that can cut through the tendency to disequilibrate. Equanimity, upekkhā, is that mental factor. It should be practiced whenever mettā, karuṇā, and muditā become inapplicable. It is also a conclusive factor within this group of noble practices, for it expresses the equal balance between self and other that lies at the heart of the other three.

To illustrate the four noble states of mind, we use the example of a mother with four children—an infant and three successively older children. The mother wants the infant to grow up to be healthy, strong, and happy. Her wishes for the baby correspond to loving-kindness, mettā. Now, let's say, the next child happens to be weak and sickly. The mother will wish him to be cured and relieved. This is compassion, karuṇā. The next child—a daughter—has come of age. She enjoys good health, follows her parents' advice, and is doing well in society. As the mother watches this child's progress, she feels happy and rejoices in her success. This is sympathetic joy, muditā. Now as for the oldest child, he is quite grown up. Infancy is long behind him; he has no particular difficulties or diseases. He can stand on his own two feet and no longer requires help and protection from the mother. She no longer needs to support him with her mettā, karuṇā, or muditā. She need not worry about his welfare—whatever happens, he's capable of taking care of himself.

This is the mature attitude of upekkhā. There is a sense of relief in acknowledging that each being must face his or her situation. One has done what one can, just as the mother once gave her best effort to raising her oldest child. But now that he is grown, it is no longer appropriate to meddle in his affairs.

Even when beings are not apparently self-sufficient, sometimes there is actually nothing more one can do. At that time, upekkhā is the appropriate attitude. It is important to note that there is no diminishment of goodwill. Suppose a man has committed a crime.

Before he's sentenced, we extend mettā and karuṇā toward him as much as possible. But once the sentence has been declared, it is time for upekkhā. There's nothing more we can do for the criminal; nor should we continue to criticize him. We can reflect, "He has to suffer the consequences of the crime he committed. He's paying his debt to society. We hope he will learn from the situation and not have too many problems in prison, so that he can emerge as a productive member of society."

If a person has not committed any visible wrong in recent existence, he or she can still experience suffering due to actions committed in an earlier existence. In Pāḷi this doctrine is known as *kammassakāta sammā-diṭṭhi,* meaning kamma is one's own inheritance. Sooner or later, one will bear the consequences of whatever one has done in the past. Reflecting on this is part of equanimity meditation; it brings a balanced perspective.

Faked equanimity also exists. Some people go around saying they possess equanimity or balance of mind at all times, everywhere and under all circumstances. If you look closely, they usually seem indifferent or uncaring. They don't want to feel too badly about their unwholesome deeds, nor are they truly eager to perform wholesome ones. As human beings, we must continually exert ourselves toward wholesomeness, and keep watch over our true intentions.

## The Method of Developing Mettā

The method for developing mettā is much the same as the methods for the other brahmacariyās. We will explain mettā bhāvanā, then, as a basic example; and we will also briefly describe the theme of protective meditations.

The basic method for mettā bhāvanā is simple. One deliberately generates wishes for others' welfare and happiness. Identifying one's own wish to be happy, one recognizes that others feel just the same way. A desire to help them arises; and so one goes out and does whatever helpful things one can. Helpful actions are a form of mettā, known as *kāya-kamma mettā,* friendly actions performed with the body. True loving-kindness includes kāya-kamma mettā and two other forms of mettā: *vacī-kamma mettā,* verbal acts of mettā; and *mano-kamma mettā,* friendly mental actions.

### *Four Kinds of Loving Speech*

To speak friendly words, recite suttas, give good advice, or simply to speak in a friendly, beneficial manner—all are forms of vacī-kamma mettā.

The specific teachings on skillful speech, *vacī-sucarita,* indicate that for speech to be skillful it must be motivated by loving-kindness. Thus, to practice skillful speech is vacī-kamma mettā.

The first type of skillful speech is truthful speech. One wishes to inform the other person honestly, so he or she may have correct understanding and knowledge. This is a wholesome, kind intention. Honesty is a form of loving-kindness.

Second, one chooses words that are unifying rather than divisive. Not only is the intent based in mettā but the result of such speech is sure to be a further expression of loving-kindness.

Third, we choose words that are sweet and pleasing, not rough, harsh language. We want to make people happy when they hear us talking. At the same time, we guard against deceit and flattery, which contain an element of dishonesty.

The fourth type of vacī-sucarita is speaking of meaningful, essential things. Not wanting to waste the other person's time, we offer worthwhile information and understanding.

People who practice vacī-sucarita will easily find friends and support. Should they become leaders, they must not suddenly abandon the principles of skillful speech. Leaders will be trusted and respected if they do not lie to the public, if they speak in a way that builds trust and friendship, if they refrain from speaking roughly or threateningly, and if they make speeches that are pithy and meaningful.

Vacī-sucarita is important in all kinds of organizations and groups—families, businesses, communities, governments. It is especially crucial in the religious arena, given that skillful speech is based on *cetanā-mettā,* or kind intention. When people sense cetanā-mettā in a religious figure they become devoted; but if kind intent is lacking, they won't want to hear anything else. As soon as a religious leader indulges in wrongful or deliberately deceptive speech, it's the beginning of the end. So long as their lies remain concealed, leaders may retain some followers, but when the truth is exposed they will undergo a public downfall.

People who love to gossip and pass around divisive tidbits often claim they just want to be kind and helpful, but this is untrue. Similarly, rough, coarse language and frivolous time-wasting chatter reveal a dearth of mettā. In general, ill-intentioned speech, *vacī-duccarita,* turns people away. People are attracted to speech that is truthful, meaningful, unifying, and friendly.

Vacī-sucarita, skillful speech, and vacī-kamma mettā, verbal acts of loving-kindness, are beneficial for everyone. The more one practices them, the more power one will have to gather others together into a respectful and supportive group. The kind intentions must be genuine, though.

### *Mental Kindness*

The third and final form of mettā is mano-kamma mettā, acts of loving-kindness performed by the mind. Essentially this means wishing others to be well and happy. Mano-kamma mettā can be radiated at all times, in all postures. It can occur as a spontaneous wish or a deliberately repeated phrase like "May she (or he, or they) be happy." To recite verbal formulas silently in the mind is the method of formal mettā meditation, which can develop one's loving-kindness to an extraordinary level. It will be described extensively below.

### *Loving-Kindness as a Protective Practice*

Mettā bhāvanā has two possible goals. It can be used to gain the *jhānas,* or absorptions, states of very strong concentration; or it can be used as a guardian meditation, leading to freedom from danger and enmity.

The technique for developing jhānic concentration has many fine points that we will not go into here, since our emphasis is on developing the insight knowledges through satipaṭṭhāna vipassanā meditation. Sufficient moment-to-moment concentration arises in satipaṭṭhāna vipassanā practice to fulfill the Noble Eightfold Path and lead to freedom from the defilements.

The protective form of mettā bhāvanā is extremely beneficial. It generates wholesome mental states, guards against inner and outer dangers and disturbances, and develops the perfections according to the example of the Buddha.

There are enemies, *vera;* and there is also fear, *bhaya.* The two are related, for if we are not free from enemies we endure danger and fear. We already distinguished outer and inner enemies—puggalā vera, the enemy that comes in the form of a person, and akusala vera and kilesa vera, unwholesomeness and mental defilements. Outer enemies are encountered relatively rarely, while the inner enemies attack us night and day, unless we protect ourselves with meditation.

Dosa is an internal enemy, as is rāga, or lust, which so often poses as mettā. When dosa and rāga arise in the stream of consciousness they disturb it; they also have the potential to bring disaster to oneself and others. Hatred, when indulged, hardens into resentment. Lust too can grow into a destructive passion. Whenever a destructive mental state is present, the mind becomes rough, coarse, wild, heavy, closed, disgusting, and dreadful. In contrast, a mind filled with mettā is peaceful, lovable, light, and open.

## *The First Wish of Mettā Meditation*

To be free from hatred and lust is *avera,* to lack an enemy. This wonderful state is the first wish we generate toward others in formal mettā bhāvanā. "May he or she be free from enemies," we say to ourselves, thinking of both inner and outer enemies. (It is all right to vary the verbal formula slightly, as long as the essence of the wish remains. For instance, the phrase you use could be "May he or she be free from danger" or "May he or she be free from enmity, danger, and fear.")

People often ask, When one meditates by radiating mettā to other beings, will these others become peaceful? This is not certain. What *is* certain is that one's own internal enemies, dosa and rāga, will be pacified and one will become peaceful oneself.

If we practice loving-kindness, it will certainly arise. If we keep at it, our mettā will gradually increase, growing powerful enough to quell the internal enemies of hatred and greed. Once these enemies are subdued, one is no longer so quick to respond to others in an angry or self-centered way—for example, by immediately forming negative judgments of those we meet, or by feeling jealous and suspicious of family members. Generally if one does not radiate mettā, or if one's practice is weak, one remains easy prey for hatred, greed, lust, and so forth. One can end up violating the precepts by killing, stealing, verbal unkindness, sexual misconduct, or intoxication.

### *Protection from Inner and Outer Danger*

Wrongdoing results from a tormented mind; it also leads to further dangers. By protecting us against inner enemies, mettā bhāvanā also averts the dangers that result from wrongdoing. These dangers are:

1. *Attānuvāda-bhaya,* the fear or danger of self-blame, feeling ashamed and guilty about what one has done.
2. *Parānuvāda-bhaya,* the fear of censure by others, losing the respect and support of people who have good judgment. Kind, ethical people tend to avoid those who habitually indulge in wrongdoing.
3. *Daṇḍa-bhaya,* fear of punishment by the authorities. If one kills, steals, lies, takes intoxicants, and is generally unruly, sooner or later this will lead to conflict with the secular authorities.
4. *Duggati-bhaya,* fear of being reborn in an unfavorable existence. Just as eating unsuitable food leads to an upset stomach, anytime one acts on a defiled intention one will suffer the consequences.

Clearly, no happiness arises in the mind of a person who is facing guilt, punishment, torture, and unfavorable rebirths.

### *Formula for Reciting Loving-Kindness*

The wish we are emanating, for others to be free from enemies or danger, is expressed in a short, simple phrase that encompasses all possible problems a being can face: outer and inner enemies, wrongdoing, and all of their future consequences. If this wish were to come true, the being toward whom we're directing it would be perfectly happy and calm. Since we're wishing them to be freed from inner enemies, we are also wishing they might reach ultimate liberation of mind, perfect peace and freedom.

So, as we mentally recite the formula "May this person be free from enemies," we're emanating a pure volition for their happiness. Though it's uncertain what the result of this will be for the recipient, great joy will develop in one's own mind. One begins to understand what it is like to be freed from inner enemies, oneself.

Mettā practice bestows the power to overcome *kodhummattaka,* mental madness based on hatred, colloquially called blind rage. Gripped by kodhummattaka, one goes berserk, out of control, and barely knows what one is doing. With mettā bhāvanā, one's knee-jerk responses become gentler, toned down; one's thoughts are less distorted, more humane.

People with strong mettā no longer wish disadvantages upon others. They genuinely hope for others' happiness. They can put up with being insulted; they can forgive and forget. They let go of grudges and can sacrifice their own benefit for the sake of other beings. These wise, kind, beautiful qualities all arise due to lack of hatred in the mind. As mettā grows stronger, the beauty of the mind increases. A generous, tolerant, unselfish person will also tend to be loved by others; he or she will be relatively free of puggalā vera, enemies in human form. Thus, the protective quality of mettā bhāvanā works inwardly and outwardly. It gradually tames the mind and behavior. As one's own little world is pacified, peace arises in the surrounding world.

### *Radiating Mettā*

To wish others to be free from enmity and danger is an efficient, focused way of radiating mettā. The wish, in the form of a phrase, is radiated repeatedly. Mettā can also be radiated spatially, first to those within one's home, then to those in the immediate neighborhood, and progressively to all beings in one's village, township, state, country, world, and universe.

If one's wishes are dedicated wholly to the welfare and happiness of others, mettā reaches the level of *mettā-pāramīs,* the perfected loving-kindness of a buddha. Each and every time one radiates loving-kindness, either to individuals or groups, one is protecting oneself, developing mettā-pāramīs, gaining merit, and sowing a beneficial kammic seed that will bear fruit someday. By radiating mettā hundreds or thousands of times, one protects oneself, develops mettā-pāramīs, and gains merit hundreds or thousands of times—quite a matter for rejoicing.

Radiating mettā once per second, within a minute one protects oneself, develops mettā-pāramīs, and gains merit sixty times. Radiating loving-kindness for five minutes, one develops mettā-pāramīs and gains merit three hundred times. An hour offers thirty-six hundred instances of protection, pāramīs, and merit.

But if we radiate the phrase "May so-and-so be well and happy" a thousand times and then speak roughly to that person, we cannot be said to possess real loving-kindness. After radiating loving-kindness mentally, we must also express it in verbal and bodily actions. Anytime we relate to other beings, we should do so with threefold loving-kindness—mental, verbal, and bodily acts of mettā. This point should be well noted.

Still, it is said in the texts that a single moment of radiating loving-kindness mentally is more beneficial than cooking up huge pots of rice and offering them to others in the morning, noon, and evening. The Saṁyutta Nikāya states this very clearly—radiating loving-kindness even for the time it takes to pull a cow's udder once is far better than making huge rice offerings three times a day. They're not talking about just one giant pot of rice, but three hundred giant pots in the morning, three hundred more at noon, and again three hundred gigantic rice pots in the evening! It would seem that a point is being made.

### *Self-Esteem and Human Status*

Most people hold themselves in high esteem; this is why they so easily lose patience. Impatience is a form of anger based on pride and conceit, or *māna.* Conceited ill will causes one to lose one's tolerance and humanity. One may continue to look like a human being from the outside, but one's mind and behavior resemble a hungry ghost's. If one remains just as irritable and impatient after radiating mettā, the practice has been superficial. It is a sign that one needs to practice more. Maybe then one will start being a little bit more generous and succeed in rising up to human status and eventually become a distinguished, even an outstanding, human being.

In human life it is quite possible to fulfill one's social duties, be generous, and improve one's mental states through meditation. If one can do all this, one will not be just a human being, and not just a distinguished human being, but a true human being. As such, when relating to others one will feel happy, cool, and peaceful.

### *Unselfishness, the Perfection of Loving-Kindness*

Since we are practicing mettā along the direction of developing pāramīs, it is good to delve into the meaning of this term.

*Pāramī* is translated as "perfection," but it means "noble becoming" or "the business of a noble person." When performing wholesome deeds of generosity, dāna, when observing morality *(sīla),* and especially in mettābhāvanā, it is extremely important that there be no selfish interest involved. This is the meaning of the term "noble." It has nothing to do with social class—or, rather, it expresses the Buddha's definition of what is valuable and respectable in human affairs.

When performing a generous deed, it should be done entirely for the benefit of others. Only then does it qualify as true generosity.

This is fairly obvious, since selfishness and generosity are contradictory. The commitment to maintain sīla, too, can be altruistic, since a refined morality includes the recognition that others are just as worthy of good treatment as oneself. Likewise, when radiating loving-kindness we can do so entirely for the welfare and happiness of others.

Anytime we are generous, moral, or kind, there should be no hint of selfishness in our attitude.

Wholesome acts of morality, generosity, and kindness do not, however, lead to assurance in the Dhamma. Only the insight knowledges attained in satipaṭṭhāna vipassanā meditation can give that ultimate assurance—the assurance that one has understood the truth of existence and will no longer be subjected to suffering. We have been talking about the importance of selflessness in the mettā practice. However, mettā practice does not by itself lead to the ultimate understanding of the Noble Eightfold Path, to liberation of the mind from suffering, or to what is called "assurance in the Dhamma." When it comes time to practice the Dhamma to attain stream entry, we may feel motivated by a profound wish for release from the suffering we experience in ourselves. To have a certain degree of self-interest here is fine. The texts say that this desire is perfectly legitimate. So, when practicing the Dhamma to attain stream entry, one will be working hard in hopes of being freed from wrong views, doubt, and the danger of rebirth in states of loss. There's nothing wrong with harboring some hope of success, and no harm is done to others either. We've already discussed how one's own insight meditation practice benefits other beings.

In all other areas besides this, one should guard strenuously against selfish interest and instead focus on benefiting others. This is a noble aim; a person who undertakes such noble activity is also called *pāramī*. Persons worthy of the title *pāramī* will act from genuine loving-kindness and compassion. They are not hoping to gain name and fame or a long life—nor even to be freed from the cycle of birth and death, saṃsāra. Their motivation is altruistic.

## Detailed Explanation of Mettā Bhāvanā

### *The Instruction for Practice*

Traditional mettā bhāvanā consists of silently repeating the following four phrases again and again:

> Sabbe sattā averā hontu
> Avyāpajjhā hontu
> Anīghā hontu
> Sukhī attānaṁ pariharantu
>
> May all beings be free from enmity and danger
> Be free from mental suffering
> Be free from physical suffering
> Care for themselves happily

When we wish to carry out a session of mettā meditation practice, the texts suggest a structure of four phrases. We begin with the phrase discussed earlier, "May all beings be free from enmity and danger." This is a clear and simple wish for others' welfare, happiness, peace, and safety.

The second line, "May all beings be free from mental suffering," offers a new twist. Again we are wishing that others may be freed from suffering, but this time we're focusing on the internal level. We wish all beings to have happiness and peace by no longer undergoing the pangs of difficult thoughts and emotions, or mental suffering in any form. *Vyāpajjha* means the pain of anger in the mind, the anger that often arises when circumstances are difficult or unpleasant. This includes all worries, all sadness, fears, grief, and separation from near and dear ones, which can bring sorrow or lamentation. Included here, too, are all the sorrows arising from worldly troubles, like businesses that fail.

In order to be truly freed from all mental suffering, beings must be freed from the internal enemy, kilesa vera. The second mettā phrase addresses this issue. We're hoping not only that beings never have to suffer pain within their minds, but also that they shall experience liberation from all the causes of mental suffering, namely, the internal afflictions. The kilesas are also the causes of destructive behavior, so by extension we're wishing that all beings could maintain ethical, cultured, compassionate behavior. Sweeping implications are condensed into a brief phrase. We're also really intending all this for the benefit of others, not hoping that the rest of the world will start behaving more civilly toward us and give us what we want.

The third line expresses a desire for all beings to be free from physical suffering. This covers all the gradations of bodily pain, anything sharp or unpleasant. We wish others to be free from diseases, wounds, pains, aches, accidents, and so on. Again there is no selfish aspect to this, no secondary hope for one's own health somehow to improve as a result of this meditation.

The final line is a wish for others to be able to look after themselves happily, to be able to bear the burdens of life with ease, to meet the requirements of their bodies and minds without hardship. It can also be translated as wishing for others to meet with supportive circumstances. Taking care of one's own body and mind is a demanding task, and we hope that all beings will receive whatever they need to sustain their lives and even leave them with enough time and mental ease so they can devote themselves to meditation practice. To speak colloquially, we want everyone to have it really good.

## Mettā Multiplication—the 528 Kinds

It's relatively easy to radiate loving-kindness in a general manner toward all beings whom one encounters, wishing them all to be well and happy. There exists a more strenuous method of developing loving-kindness, known as the 528 kinds of mettā.

### *Nonspecific Radiation: Four Kinds of Mettā*

We spoke of the traditional four phrases. Each one of these four lines of the mettā bhāvanā recitation can be thought of as one particular kind of loving-kindness. "Sabbe sattā avera hontu—may all beings be free from enmity and danger" is one form loving-kindness can take. "Avyāpajjhā hontu—may they be free from mental pain" is another flavor, if you will, that amounts to wishing for others' internal happiness. "Anīghā hontu—may they be free from physical problems" is yet another way of wishing for others' well-being.

Once a person is generally happy and has been freed from mental and physical suffering, things seem to be getting pretty good. "Sukhī attānaṁ pariharantu—may all beings be able to look after themselves happily" extends our loving-kindness yet further. It may seem a luxurious expression of loving-kindness. Yet looking after one's body is a huge task that beings are forced to assume. A body has to be fed, its bowels have to be moved, it has to be rested and cleaned. Keeping up with the body is a form of suffering. Wishing another being to be able to look after his or her own body happily is, in fact, a profound expression of mettā.

These four lines of mettā bhāvanā are directed to all beings. This is called "nonspecific radiation."

### *Unlimited Radiation: Twenty Kinds of Mettā*

In order to multiply the types of mettā, we direct our loving-kindness to different types of beings. We have sent our wishes to *sabbe sattā,* "all beings." To this large group we add four more general categories: *sabbe pāṇā,* "all breathing beings"; *sabbe bhūtā,* "all beings who have been born"; *sabbe puggalā,* "all individual beings"; and *sabbe attabhāvā pariyāpannā,* "all beings contained in bodies, who possess materiality and mentality."

We radiate mettā to all these kinds of beings, group by group, via the four phrases. As we have already dealt with the first group, all beings, we will have completed five basic categorizations. Each group has received four phrases, so we have radiated a total of twenty types of mettā.

The five categories are called *anodiso pharana mettā,* "unlimited radiation of loving-kindness" (the word *pharaṇa* can also translate as suffusion or pervasion). Mettā is being radiated to all these beings.

## *Specific Radiation: Twenty-Eight Kinds of Mettā*

We have not yet divided the groups into categories. Now we will place beings in categories by gender, by spiritual realization, and by the realm of existence they inhabit. Each of these general categories has its own subdivisions, ending up with a total of seven categories.

We distinguish two genders, females and males, and send mettā to all of each. *Sabbā itthiyo,* "all females," includes not just human women but all female beings in the universe. *Sabbe purisā,* "all males," refers not just to human men but to all male beings in this universe.

The spiritual realization category is also divided into two. We send mettā to all the noble beings who have realized the Dhamma—*sabbe ariyā;* and then to all those beings who have not yet realized the Dhamma—*sabbe anariyā,* "non-noble beings." Non-noble beings are also known as puthujjanas, ordinary worldlings, still chained by suffering and a full degree of ignorance.

The realms of existence are divided into three levels. *Sabbe devā,* "all celestial beings," are those who live in the higher realms, deva and Brahma beings. *Sabbe manussā* includes all human beings. *Sabbe vinipātikā* refers to all beings who have fallen into miserable states of existence from which it is difficult to escape, the realms of animals, hungry ghosts, and hell beings. These are also called *apāya,* states of loss.

We send mettā via the original four lines to the beings in each of these seven categories of existence. "May all (these beings) be free from enmity, from mental suffering, physical suffering, and be able to care for themselves." At this point we have sent out twenty-eight more forms of mettā.

Because we are specifically radiating loving-kindness to specific, separate groups, this set of phrases (practice) is called *odiso pharaṇa mettā,* the specific pervasion or suffusion of loving-kindness. Adding the twenty-eight new kinds of odiso pharaṇa mettā to the twenty kinds of nonspecific pervasion *(anodiso pharaṇa mettā),* we have accumulated forty-eight types of mettā so far.

### *Ten Directions: 480 Kinds of Mettā*

Next, we send out mettā to all these categories of beings in the ten directions. There is a particular order as follows—first the principal directions of the compass, east, west, north, south; then the intermediate directions, northeast, southeast, northwest, southwest; and then to all beings in the lower direction and then in the upper direction, the zenith. If we radiate mettā to each of the 48 categories above, in all of the 10 directions, we have 480 kinds of mettā. "May all females to the north be free from enmity and danger," etc.

Add these 480 types of mettā to the 48 that were sent out before we started pervading the universe directionally, and we have the grand total of 528 types of mettā.

### *Mettā Practice Session*

And so let us now radiate loving-kindness to all beings. Let us do this together with all meditators and Dhamma friends.

> May all beings be free from enmity and danger,
> be free from mental suffering,
> be free from physical suffering,
> and be able to look after themselves happily.
> May all breathing beings be free from enmity and danger,
> be free from mental suffering,
> be free from physical suffering,
> and be able to look after themselves happily.
> May all beings who have been born be free from enmity and danger,
> be free from mental suffering,
> be free from physical suffering,
> and be able to look after themselves happily.
> May all individuals be free from enmity and danger,
> be free from mental suffering,
> be free from physical suffering,
> and be able to look after themselves happily.

May all those who are contained in bodies be free from
enmity and danger,
be free from mental suffering,
be free from physical suffering,
and be able to look after themselves happily.
May all female beings be free from enmity and danger,
be free from mental suffering,
be free from physical suffering,
and be able to look after themselves happily.
May all male beings be free from enmity and danger,
be free from mental suffering,
be free from physical suffering,
and be able to look after themselves happily.
May all noble ones…
May all non-noble ones, the worldlings…
May all celestial beings…
May all human beings…
May all beings in states of loss be free from enmity and danger,
be free from mental suffering,
be free from physical suffering,
and be able to look after themselves happily.

So we have just performed the twenty kinds of nonspecific radiation of loving-kindness, anodiso pharaṇa mettā, and the twenty-eight kinds of specific radiating of mettā, odiso pharaṇa mettā. Together these make forty-eight. So far, they are nondirectional.

As for the directional type of loving-kindness, it would take too many pages to radiate forty-eight categories in all ten directions. So let us simply radiate mettā to all beings.

# 4 *Liberating the Mind with Direct Knowledge, Satipaṭṭhāna Vipassanā*

## Listening to Dhamma Vinaya

The Buddha taught for forty-five years. On the night of his death he called his attendant, Ānanda, and told him, "Dhamma Vinaya shall now be your teacher."

Explanations of the term Dhamma are many, but of Vinaya are few; the combined term receives very little attention. In general, Dhamma means doing what is beneficial, while Vinaya means letting go of what is not beneficial. According to Venerable Mahāsi Sayādaw, Dhamma consists of teachings for the welfare of all beings, while Vinaya is the law, discipline, and regulations. *Vinaya* means "that which shapes the behavior of beings so that it is beautiful." Unless we consciously shape our physical, verbal, and mental behavior, it will be ugly.

The Buddha prohibited killing, stealing, sexual abuse, lying, and intoxication because of the grave consequences arising from all of these actions. He encouraged kindness, generosity, morality, and mental cultivation because of their incalculable benefits. All genuine spiritual teachers must know what is beneficial and not beneficial for beings. Out of knowledge and compassion, they must exhort students to do what is beneficial and give up what is not.

### *A Liberating Gift*

Dhamma Vinaya is present in every religion to some extent, but the complete teachings of the Buddha are unique. The complete doctrine is held in the Tipiṭaka, the Three Baskets, so called because the scriptures are grouped as if into baskets. The first two are known as the Dhamma Piṭakas; they are the Sutta Piṭaka, the Buddha's discourses; and the Abhidhamma Piṭaka, the analysis of mind and mental states. The third Piṭaka is the Vinaya Piṭaka, the book of discipline.

The suttas express the Buddha's omniscient knowledge and compassion. The Abhidhamma is wisdom, paññā. The Vinaya is pure compassion.

In Burma, Dhamma Vinaya is not considered a religion. The Pāḷi word is *sāsana,* often translated as "dispensation." That translation combines the meanings of a gift and deliverance—Dhamma Vinaya was dispensed freely; and it dispenses us from suffering. "Dispensation" is a good term but awkward. A more workable translation of *sāsana* would probably be "teaching."

The Buddha's teaching, if we undertake it, leads out of suffering. It is indeed a gift to be cherished and put into practice. The Buddha's sāsana always leads to purity and to refined and cultured behavior of body, speech, and mind. If we follow it, we can claim our true heritage as human beings.

## *A Complete Teaching*

Buddha *vācana,* the speech of the Buddha, was directed solely to the purification of beings, to the overcoming of defilement and affliction. His speech was all teaching, in which he explained and encouraged beings to cultivate morality, concentration, and wisdom. By means of these three trainings we can achieve something that has not been achieved before in ourselves, a new and extraordinary unprecedented state which indeed cannot be achieved by any other means.

Sīla sikkhā, the training in morality, overcomes defilements of the body. Samādhi sikkhā, training in concentration, purifies the mind. Paññā sikkhā, training in wisdom, roots out the latent defilements. Nothing is left out, but one must cultivate all parts. If not, one will be overcome by gross, medium, and subtle defilements for the rest of one's life, and possibly be reborn in an unfortunate situation.

If you practice Dhamma Vinaya, Dhamma Vinaya will save you.

It prevents beings from falling into states of loss. It extinguishes the *āsava kilesa,* the defilements that flow into the mind uninvited and cause us to misperceive reality. Under the influence of āsava kilesas, we indulge in behavior that harms ourselves and others. We don't realize that one hundred percent of all suffering is caused by mental defilements, burning and dragging us down. To indulge in them leads to wrongdoing and a lowering of status. One loses humanity, not to mention happiness.

Eradicating defilements is the goal. This is equivalent to nibbāna. If you don't practice the complete training, with nibbāna as your goal, sooner or later you will suffer. But if you really try hard to get rid of the defilements, you will come to enjoy a cultured, cool, and cultivated life.

### *Fulfilling the Training*

*Sāsana sampatti* is a Pāḷi term meaning that a person has fulfilled or perfected the Buddha's training, sāsana. Her behavior is cultured, her speech is truthful and sweet, her mind calm and free. A secondary implication of fulfillment is that this fully cultured, refined person is imbued with satisfaction and contentment. Of course, this satisfaction isn't based on becoming more judgmental of others and thinking oneself superior. This happiness can result only from self-discipline and training.

The first step is to listen respectfully to Dhamma advice with the aim of carrying out the training described. As we listen, we endeavor to commit to memory the advice being given, so that we can carry out the practice faithfully on our own. By closely following the teachings, we will perfect the teaching within ourselves, sāsana sampatti.

Thus, having heard or read about the principles of morality, we resolve to understand, remember, and put morality into practice. To practice sīla means giving up the transgressive defilements. Certain things are no longer done nor said.

This establishes sīla sāsana, the teaching of morality, within oneself. A person who fulfills sīla is a high-class person, regardless of how much or little money or education he or she may have. He is flawless, cultivated, refined. Morality also keeps a person free from worries and remorse—bright, light, and uplifted within.

Examining this matter closely, however, we must admit it isn't enough just to say we are going to be nicer and give up our bad habits. We need mental training. Without it, sooner or later, some impulse based on ill will, greed, or delusion will overpower us and we'll commit unworthy acts. Alas, this is inevitable.

One must control the mind through meditation. Without the focused, accurate awareness of satipaṭṭhāna vipassanā, whenever a lovely or horrid or poorly observed object comes along, then the corresponding kilesa of lust or hate or ignorance will becloud the mind. If we're noting and observing everything, however, objects will be clearly seen. No kilesas will arise and we can respond with aplomb.

Listen carefully to the meditation method, then do your best to carry it out. With faithful practice you will establish the attainment of concentration, samādhi sampatti, within your mind-body continuum. With effort, one gains fulfillment. One observes the body, feelings, the mind, and all other objects—the four foundations of mindfulness. When one pays attention to the body, it is said that the instruction of the first establishment, *kāyānupassanā satipaṭṭhāna,* is fulfilled. Observing pleasant, unpleasant, and neutral feelings, the second establishment of *vedanānupassanā satipaṭṭhāna* is fulfilled. By attending to the mind one performs the third establishment of *cittānupassanā satipaṭṭhāna.* By paying attention to general actions one fulfills the instruction of the fourth establishment, *dhammānupassanā satipaṭṭhāna.* It is by continuous effort at all six sense doors that one can fulfill the four establishments of mindfulness.

Do not be daunted! It sounds complex, but really only one kind of effort is needed to succeed at this kind of meditation. You must try repeatedly to aim the mind at the object. This means doggedly returning the mind to the object whenever it strays, plus a continual effort to upgrade the quality of your observation. Then you will come to know the nature of the object and begin experiencing the successive phases of vipassanā insight knowledge. Finally, you will reach nibbāna and uproot the latent defilements.

With help from vipassanā paññā, insight wisdom or knowledge, one suppresses the defilements and is fulfilled with wisdom, paññā sampatti. When paññā sampatti is nurtured repeatedly over a period of time, one becomes a noble person, an outstanding human being. Such a person, we say, has gained the Dhamma. He or she has claimed the highest heritage of a human being.

To follow Dhamma Vinaya, we accept the Buddha's advice to stay within certain bounds. By listening carefully and respectfully, remembering and taking to heart the teachings, we become a true disciple. The Pāḷi word for a disciple, *sāvaka,* means "listener." Please be as good a sāvaka as you can.

## The Depth of Dhamma Vinaya

The hermit Sumedha could have become a fully liberated arahant, enjoying the bliss of nibbāna for many eons before his birth in our own historical period. But seeing the suffering of others, he gave up his chance in order to fulfill the arduous, lengthy task of developing his perfections, beginning with dāna, generosity.

After many existences and many experiences, at last his qualities were mature. Then, the Buddha-to-be renounced the world and undertook satipaṭṭhāna vipassanā meditation. He progressed through the insight knowledges one by one until he'd gained all four *magga* and *phala,* the path and fruition knowledges, of the stream-enterer, once-returner, nonreturner, and arahant. *Arahatta magga phala,* the path and fruition of holiness, was the culmination of his practice. Due to his overwhelming pāramī, he also simultaneously dispelled all of his *vāsanā,* or kammic tendencies, and obtained omniscient knowledge. Thus he became a fully enlightened Buddha.

He uprooted suffering by extinguishing the mental pollutants of greed, hatred, and delusion. Arahants, too, extinguish these, but there's a difference. An arahant's attainment of Dhamma kills off the defilements, and yet some traces of the vāsanās remain. For example, a being who had previously displayed hatred in the form of rough, insulting speech might still occasionally speak abusively after becoming an arahant, but there will no longer be any unwholesome intent behind it. A hint of dosa tendency—or of other bad habits he or she once had—will linger. A being who accumulated proud, conceited behavior for a long time might still seem arrogant after attaining arahantship, but again the unwholesome intent will be lacking. The vāsanā left behind in an arahant is like a strong smell remaining in a bottle. In a bottle used to store alcohol, the scent of alcohol often remains even after many rinsings. So it is with the minds of arahants.

The Buddha, however, exhausted all the kilesas along with all his past tendencies. This is the meaning of the expression "without remainder" when it is said that he "eradicated the kilesas without remainder."

No matter how many lovely, greed-inducing objects he might have encountered, the Buddha never responded with the slightest greed, liking, or wanting. Faced with unpleasant, dosa-inducing objects, he never gave rise to ill will, hatred, or aversion. Moha-inducing objects could not induce bewilderment or confusion in him. The Buddha was completely unconfused. He knew everything with sabbaññutā-ñāṇa.

The hermit Sumedha's long efforts fulfilled *hetu-sampadā,* the attainment of the cause of buddhahood. By gaining the Dhamma of arahantship and omniscience he fulfilled *phala-sampadā,* or attainment of the fruit. Then he completed his compassionate intent (and fulfilled Dipankara's prophecy) by setting forth to share the Dhamma with others, *sattupakāra-sampadā.*

In this world, some people try to reap the effects without fulfilling the causes. They are known as opportunists. Others work to fulfill causes, and even receive the effects, but then do not go out and work for others. Despite their great success, these people are despised as misers. The Buddha was neither opportunistic nor miserly. He fulfilled cause and effect; then he taught. His work was completely satisfactory.

No one else could have done the work he did. For forty-five years he strove to help human, celestial, and Brahma beings. He made it possible for each class of beings to reach happiness according to their pāramīs: human happiness for humans, celestial happiness for celestial beings, Brahma happiness for Brahma beings.

Meditation teachers in our own time should contemplate his example. Before teaching others, the Buddha shaped himself first. His success was spectacular and fully earned. All teachers should make sure they are well shaped and well behaved before going out to serve the public. If a teacher cannot even maintain a basic level of morality, he or she will be justly targeted for criticism. To shape one's own behavior is also crucial in order to experience human happiness.

## Equal Opportunity for All

The Buddha's Dhamma Vinaya is impartial and unbiased. It creates no hierarchy among ordinary worldlings, the *puthujjana.* Anyone who practices this Dhamma without expecting preferential treatment will be able to realize it. This assurance can be given. The Buddha reached the top and won people's respect by eradicating defilements and gaining purity. His teaching shows how to follow in his footsteps, no more and no less.

Consider the practice of sīla, morality. When young people uphold sīla, they gain purity of physical and verbal behavior. When middle-aged people practice the precepts, they too gain purity. When elderly people keep the precepts, again it is no different. The fruits of morality are available to all people at all stages of life, whatever group they may belong to. Everyone can gain refinement.

Similarly, satipaṭṭhāna vipassanā suppresses the kilesas in the mind of the one who practices. When mindfulness is present and continuous, defilements can't intervene. The mind becomes concentrated: samādhi will arise. These experiences are not given preferentially to some while being withheld from others. Of course, one must be practicing correctly, putting in the requisite effort, following the teacher's instructions. Give it a fair try, though; you'll see results.

If a meditator keeps aiming the mind at the object of observation, he or she will eventually begin to attain the progressive insight knowledges beginning with the ability to distinguish between mind *(nāma)* and matter *(rūpa).* Then he or she will be able to see the operation of cause and effect and come to understand the universal characteristics of impermanence, suffering, and nonself. If this meditator continues to practice, he or she will progress through the various insight knowledges all the way up to the cool happiness of nibbāna. No preference is given to anyone in this sequence. Even if, due to insufficient time in retreat or some other issue, one is unable to complete the sequence of insight knowledges and attain stream entry, still it is inevitable that one will receive benefits. Meanwhile, there will be no harm passed on to others. Is this not completely fair and balanced?

In the Dhamma, women and men receive equal treatment. The Buddha's Dhamma Vinaya offers equal opportunities for all.

## Four Necessary Factors for Success in Dhamma Practice

To be successful in Dhamma Vinaya, four factors must be present at the outset:

First, it is necessary to approach and associate with a genuine teacher, one who can teach the correct Dhamma in accordance with the Buddha's instructions. This is *sappurisa-saṃseva.* Some people whom we approach for guidance may or may not be able to give correct advice. If we do find someone who can give correct advice, this person becomes a spiritual friend, *kalyāṇa mitta,* for us.

The second factor is to listen to these correct guidelines, instructions, and advice—or to read up on them. This is *saddhamma savaṇa,* or correct Dhamma study.

After this, naturally, the third factor is to take to heart the advice given. Furthermore, we must direct our minds toward maintaining upright, straightforward behavior no matter what comes up in ordinary life or during meditation. This is *yoniso-mānasikāra,* a stable mind in all circumstances.

The fourth factor is to resolve, "I will follow the Dhamma advice as it is given." This is known as *dhammānudhamma paṭipatti,* practice of Dhamma in accordance with the Dhamma.

All these factors must be present at the time of listening to the Dhamma Vinaya.

## The Example of King Milinda—How to Approach the Teachings

King Milinda was a Greek regent in Northwest India, during the first century B.C. When he became interested in Buddhist teachings, he pursued his interest by approaching the monastic Saṅgha, in particular a monk called Elder Nāgasena, and asking a series of penetrating questions. Although he was a king, he approached monks respectfully and sat down in the position of a disciple. King Milinda was serious and careful in every way during his pursuit of Dhamma understanding.

In forming a question, his mental intention was *ñātukāma,* a desire to acquire knowledge. He also had *sotukāma,* a wish to hear the precious Dhamma. After listening to the Dhamma he would not immediately forget it for he had *dhāretukāma,* the intention to remember what he had heard.

He desired the light of wisdom, *ñāṇālokaṃ daṭṭukāma.* He wished to dispel ignorance and unknowing, *añāṇaṃbhinditukāma.* He intended to find the light of knowledge, *ñāṇālokaṃ uppādetukāma.* King Milinda's ultimate objective was to destroy the darkness of avijjā, ignorance or delusion, *avijjandhakāraṁ nāsetukāma.* Avijjā is like darkness.

When one is in darkness one sees little or nothing. If one knows a little, even that little is distorted. It is like a person who suffers from a cataract who not only sees less than a normal person but sees everything as a blur. King Milinda had a strong desire to clear his inner vision.

In approaching the Saṅgha, King Milinda had extreme stability of mind. He possessed strong effort *(viriya),* much courage, and a great reflective and discriminative power. These qualities are necessary for all meditators who approach a teacher. King Milinda may be of particular interest for Westerners since he is one of the first recorded examples of a convert who subjected Buddhism to a rigorous inquiry from the Greek—fundamentally the Western—point of view. His dialogues with Elder Nāgasena are recorded in a book, *The Questions of King Milinda,* or *Milinda Panhā* in Pāḷi.

## Qualities Needed during Meditation Practice

The crux of meditation practice is to sustain continuous mindfulness. For this one needs stability and durability of mind, strong effort, and the courage to overcome difficulties—the same qualities that King Milinda brought to bear upon his own investigations.

Moreover, a meditator needs discernment *(sampajañña).* She or he must be capable of assessing what will be suitable, as opposed to what will be distracting or otherwise deleterious to the continuity of mindfulness. In deciding whether to undertake an activity, then, a meditator must reflect wisely, make a decision, and stick to it.

Some meditators allow gaps to arise in their mindfulness. These people must try to revive their good qualities, and resume. Durability of mind, effort, courage, and discrimination can never be slack or halfhearted. We need extraordinary durability, extraordinary effort, extraordinary courage, and extraordinary discernment.

## The Liberating Practice of Satipaṭṭhāna Vipassanā Meditation

Our meditative tradition was founded by the late Venerable Mahāsi Sayādaw of Rangoon. According to his instructions, satipaṭṭhāna vipassanā, also known as insight meditation, is the primary teaching. Discourses on mettā are also offered, though far less often. This is because insight wisdom has the capacity to liberate the mind by seeing the Dhamma directly.

Unfortunately, however, not everyone can practice high-level satipaṭṭhāna vipassanā. It is a demanding practice, suitable for a minority of exceptional people.

The benefits to be gained from this type of meditation, furthermore, are primarily for oneself. Others do benefit, but this happens somewhat indirectly. Since mettā is easier for most people to develop and it benefits everyone, the practice of loving-kindness really ought to become widespread. But if we undertake the practice of mettā, we must never lose sight of the unique possibilities offered by vipassanā meditation.

## Basic Instructions for Satipaṭṭhāna Vipassanā Meditation

### *Posture*

Any basic sitting posture is all right, whether the legs are crossed or folded. One can be sitting in a chair, but if so, the back should not be supported. The body should be as upright as possible and the eyes should be closed (unless you are drowsy).

### *Primary Object*

The main object of awareness is the natural breath, as it is. Do not try to control the breath in any way, simply allow it to come and go while closely observing what happens in the area of the abdomen. The rising of the abdomen along with the in-breath, and the falling of the abdomen along with the out-breath, will consist of a variety of sensations and experiences. All of these should be noticed as continuously as possible. Let there be no gaps in your attention.

The observation of any object has three parts:

1. Occurrence: attention should arrive quickly, as close to the arising of the object as possible.
2. Labeling and observation: label the rising movement of the observer as "rising," and the falling as "falling." Observation of the object should be careful and diligent, the label gentle and simple. It is not necessary to form elaborate concepts of what is going on. Labeling merely identifies the event and serves to direct the mind toward it.
3. Knowing the nature: in rising and falling of the abdomen, one knows the sensations as they are. In the rising, for example, there are likely to be sensations of tension, tightness, stiffness, and hardness. There can also be vibration and movement.

It is not possible to observe the rising and falling continuously for a very long time. Other objects will arise; when they do, it is often recommended to move the attention away from the breath.

### *How to Deal with Other Objects*

Numerous other objects can be the focus of attention.

1. Eventually the mind wanders. When this happens, shift attention to the wandering and take it as a new object. Label it, but do not get attached to the content of the thoughts. This is very important. The thoughts may disappear right away, in which case you return to the rising and falling. The thoughts may also seem great and fascinating, or else horribly absorbing. No matter how thoughts appear, all of them resemble soap bubbles. Try not to jump onto a train of thoughts and get completely lost!

   If the wandering mind persists and you become thoroughly

absorbed and distracted, cut off your involvement in thinking and return to the sensations at the abdomen.

Minor or background thinking is to be ignored.

2. Pain will arise in the body. When these sensations become predominant, let go of the rising and falling. Label the pain as "pain, pain" and observe it for a while. Label it again.

   There are four things to be known about physical pain: its quality or characteristic—for example, it may be burning, stabbing, piercing, tearing; its intensity—it may increase, remain the same, or decrease; its location—it may stay put, vanish, spread, or move; and its duration—it may last for a short moment or for an entire sitting, or it may blink on and off.

   Do remember that the purpose of paying attention to pain is to know its nature, not to heal it or make it go away. All the same, sometimes pain will disappear or change under close observation. On the other hand, its intensity may well increase. Any such changes are to be registered.

   Facing strong pain calls for patience and determination. Don't change your posture; instead, try to know the pain more deeply. Changing one's posture weakens concentration. If pain becomes excruciating, though, it is okay to move as long as the change of posture is carried out in full awareness.

3. Loud sound can occur. Label it "hearing" and observe the process of hearing. Notice the volume of the sound and its impact on the ear, and any mental reactions. It is not good to spend too much time on external sounds because this leads to distraction. Do not decide to take sound as a primary object.

4. Internal seeing may arise—visions and visual impressions of colors, forms, landscapes, and sights either remembered or imaginary, realistic or fantastic. Or visions of colors, forms, sights either remembered or imaginary may arise. It is to be labeled "seeing," and observed. Be careful not to get carried away with it for it can become absorbing and thrilling, and is often quite pleasant. This can become an issue for some meditators.

5. Moods or mental states—joy, sloth, hatred, and so forth—will become pervasive, strong, or predominant. Take the mood as the object; label and observe it. If it dissipates, return to the rising and falling. Often, moods and emotions will be associated with sensations in the body. If so, give preference to those sensations rather than any thoughts that may also be arising in association with the mood.

In brief one must label and observe everything. Whatever object is the most predominant at any given moment is the focus of attention. You start off with the rising and falling; initially, this develops concentration, stabilizes the mind. Later on, examining a greater array of objects builds energy and flexibility. You also return to the primary object whenever there is nothing else that is clear and easy to observe. If several objects are about the same in their intensity, simply choose one of them.

### *Mental Factors for Success*

The most important meditative factor is mindfulness. It should be continuous, ideally from the moment of waking up to the moment of falling asleep. Concentration and effort are important too. The jhānic factor of "aiming" *(vitakka)* is the knowing mind focused at the object. It is with effort *(viriya)* that we propel the mind toward the object. When the mind and object are in contact there is "rubbing" *(vicāra)*—a connected contact of attention and object. Mindfulness will arise, and so will wisdom, based on concentration.

### *Schedule on Retreat*

In the beginning of a retreat, you should sit one hour and walk one hour, more or less. Forty-five minutes of each is also fine. Later on you can sit longer and walk a bit less. On retreat, meditation lasts all day and evening. Meditators get up at four or five o'clock in the morning and stay up as late as they can, meditating. They often reduce their hours of sleep to four or even fewer. Often, too, the last meal of the day is eliminated and only tea is taken. This helps to increase the hours of practice and reduce sleepiness; it also adds wholesome volition by following the example of monks and nuns, whose precepts include foregoing the evening meal.

### *Walking Meditation Instructions*

Choose a lane or path where you can walk up and down undisturbed. Divide one hour of walking meditation into three segments.

For the first twenty minutes you can walk relatively fast. Note "left, right, left, right" while paying attention to the predominant sensations in the relevant legs and feet.

For the next twenty minutes, walk a little slower. Note "lifting, placing" or "lifting, lowering" while paying close attention only to the foot that is moving. When you note "lifting," try to have the noting and the attention coincide at exactly the moment when the heel leaves the ground. When you note "placing" or "lowering," start with the first moment of heaviness arising in the foot. Register the first touch on the ground and stick with the shift in weight until the foot is fully still. Then move your attention to the other foot, the one that is about to move.

During the final twenty minutes, walk as slowly as possible. Note "lifting, moving, placing" while paying attention to the moving foot only. The slower you go, the faster you will progress!

During walking meditation, you will be aware of sensations or movement. There may be trembling or unsteadiness, especially at first. The movement will not be continuous, and you may also experience slightly odd sensations. For example, you may feel as if you or your foot is being pushed.

Practice restraint of the senses, not looking here and there. Nor is it necessary to look at the feet; just place your gaze a little ahead of yourself, so that you can see where you are going. Sense-restraint while walking develops concentration; it also avoids unwholesome mental states not yet arisen.

### *General Activities*

Slow down all your movements on retreat. Moving super slowly is a great tactic, which helps us see many, many minute details in the body and the mind. Myriad things arise that we are usually not aware of; seeing them develops wisdom. However, if you succeed only in feeling restless, or if a torrent of thoughts develops, find a pace where your mindfulness can coordinate with your body movements.

You should be aware of all activities without exception. If there is a sound on waking, it should be noted. Notice sitting up in bed. Also be aware of meals, of taking food onto the plate, and of all the complex activities required for eating.

Continuity, restraint, and slowness will support your meditation.

### *The Interview*

In my way of teaching the interview is a crucial component. I expect a very high standard. Accuracy, brevity, and precision are the key points. Generally an interview lasts ten minutes. Make sure that you allow enough time to complete your report as well as for the teacher to ask questions and give you some instructions.

Describe the primary object according to a three-part scheme—how it occurred, how you labeled and observed it, and then what you knew or noticed about it. Do the same for the other distinct objects that arose during the session. The teacher needs to understand what is arising in your practice, how you become aware of it, and how the object is experienced once the awareness has landed on it. Remember, your entire daily biography is not needed—a trained teacher understands a great deal from a succinct report. If anything unusual happens in your practice during the day, it is also good to mention it.

Stick to the formula. Don't bring in fancy Pāḷi terms. Refrain from interpreting your own experiences. Don't report imaginary experiences—honesty and sincerity are needed.

This style of reporting has a galvanizing effect on practice.

The instructions that the teacher gives in return usually consist of just a few words.

# 5 *Technical Discussion of Satipaṭṭhāna Vipassanā Meditation*

## How the Noble Eightfold Path Is Developed in Every Moment of Noting

With every moment of noting an object, a meditator who practices satipaṭṭhāna vipassanā enters the Noble Eightfold Path, the way of release from suffering. In our tradition, as noted, the primary object of attention is the rising and falling of the abdomen due to the breathing process. Each time a meditator notes the rising and falling of the abdomen, he or she has to make an effort to reach the object. In the language of the Noble Eightfold Path, this is known as Right Effort, *sammā-vāyāma.* The effort expended allows the meditator to observe and remember the object. Distraction is reduced; one begins to be able to sustain attentive mindfulness on the object. Eventually mindfulness arises continuously. This, in the language of the Noble Eightfold Path, is Right Mindfulness, *sammā-sati.* When mindfulness is continuous and sustained, then gradually the mind will begin to stay on the object in a fixed manner. This, again in the language of the Noble Eightfold Path, is Right Concentration, *sammā-samādhi.*

With Right Effort the kilesas, or defilements, will not be accepted into the mind. Right Effort helps to block off the entrance to the so-called Path of Unwholesomeness or Path of Mental Defilements. Simultaneously, the Path of Wholesomeness opens up. Mindfulness protects the mind from attack by kilesas. Concentration has the effect of unifying and focusing the mind so that it stays on the object as and when it arises. These three mental factors—effort, mindfulness, and concentration—together are known as the *samādhi khandha,* the concentration group, which is one sector of the Noble Eightfold Path. They're also known as *samādhi sikkhā,* the training in concentration, or *samādhi sāsana,* the teaching of concentration. In ordinary shorthand we just call them *samādhi.*

When the concentration group comes together in the mind, kilesas don't stand a chance. As the meditator aims the mind again and again, his or her awareness gets more and more focused and direct. Sensuous thoughts, *kāma-vitakka,* fail to arise. Nor will there be thoughts of hatred and ill will, *vyāpāda-vitakka.* The desire to torment others, *vihiṁsā-vitakka,* will disappear. Since the mind goes straight to the object of meditation, it does not slip off into lust, distraction, and other forms of torment. The *pariyuṭṭhāna kilesa,* or obsessive mental defilements, are overcome. In one minute of practice, *sammā-sankappa,* or Right Aim, arises sixty times. Sammā-sankappa is another factor of the Noble Eightfold Path.

While noting the rising and falling of the abdomen moment by moment, one sees its nature sixty times a minute. The actual nature of the movement will be seen, understood, and known for oneself—not through the mediation of anybody else. When other objects arise, they will be known in the same way. This direct understanding is Right View, *sammā-diṭṭhi.* The two factors of sammā-sankappa and sammā-diṭṭhi, together, are called *paññā khandha,* the wisdom group of the Noble Eightfold Path. They're also called *paññā sikkhā,* the training in wisdom, or *paññā sāsana,* the teaching of wisdom. With training in wisdom, even the dormant or latent defilements, the *anusaya kilesa,* will be temporarily dispelled. Seeing the actual nature of the mind-body process, we begin to cut through to more subtle levels of knowledge.

Before taking up vipassanā meditation practice, one generally undertakes to observe the precepts. In the purified environment of a retreat it can even be difficult to break them! Whenever we are able to keep the precepts, by definition we demolish transgressive defilements, the *vīkkama kilesa.* Physical and verbal behavior are tamed, and one becomes outwardly more civilized and cultivated. When morality is present, this is called *sīla khandha,* the morality group of the Noble Eightfold Path; or *sīla sikkhā,* the training in morality, or the *sīla sāsana,* the teaching of morality. Included in sīla sikkhā are three Noble Eightfold Path Factors: Right Speech, *sammā-vācā,* Right Action, *sammā-kammanta,* and Right Livelihood, *sammā-ājīva.* By practicing meditation, one will gradually be endowed with right speech, action, and livelihood.

If we add the morality group to the concentration and wisdom groups discussed above, a meditator has fulfilled all the elements of the Noble Eightfold Path.

As transgressive behavior of body and speech diminishes, there are palpable benefits for oneself. Pain-causing actions tend to lead to their own consequences outwardly. They also give rise to painful, dangerous, and difficult thoughts inwardly. If we no longer reinforce the mental defilements by acting upon them, the vicious cycle is broken. Desires to harm others gradually fade away. As mental defilements are undermined by the practice of morality, we avoid the repercussions of our own bad behavior, and we gain tranquility and happiness while simultaneously protecting other beings. In this way, vipassanā practice qualifies as *parahita,* or work for others' benefit.

Whenever one observes presently arising objects directly—which means observing them as soon as they arise, with morality, concentration, and wisdom—then one will be free from gross, medium, and subtle or latent defilements. There will be freedom from *lobha:* craving, desire, lust, and all similar feelings. There will be freedom from dosa: hatred, anger, ill will, and their relatives. Moha—bewilderment, delusion, unclear seeing—will also be absent. When greed, hatred, and delusion are absent the mind is pure, clean, clear.

If the mind is not clear and clean, we are accepting a low standard of living, a low status. On the other hand, if the mind is pure we should think of this as a high standard of living, a high status. One's mind and behavior become refined. Freed from greed, hatred, and delusion, we are untroubled within. Everyone cherishes these qualities of refinement and calm. Here we see how meditators benefit directly from their practice. At the same time, others who live nearby will also gain indirect benefits. The meditator does not agitate his or her surroundings, and so the world becomes more peaceful for everyone.

Gaining a victory with the help of morality, concentration, and wisdom is known in the Pāḷi language as *dhamma-vijaya,* Dhamma success or Dhamma victory. When one gains this Dhamma success in one's own small world, there will be fewer problems overall. One's own mind and surroundings become cool and peaceful. We spread less harm; the world gets better for everybody.

Some people gain victory by weapons, others by the use of power. Still others manipulate groups or even threaten, frighten, and torture others. These external victories are based in greed, hatred, and delusion—lobha, dosa, and moha. They have mixed consequences at best and certainly don't qualify as Dhamma victories. Instead they're known as *adhamma* victories, that is, truthless victories. Gaining adhamma victory, one tends to lose one's integrity and dignity, and problems arise as a consequence. The Buddha has given us instead the satipaṭṭhāna vipassanā practice, a path that leads to victory over ourselves. When we have this inner victory, it is we who reap the greatest benefit.

## Powerful Mindfulness

When we practice, we need to stay within certain boundaries. The term *Dhamma Vinaya* provides a general overview of what these might be. We should do what is beneficial, and abandon what is not.

The thirty-seven *bodhipakkhiyā dhammā* contain the gist of the Dhamma. They include the four foundations of mindfulness, the four forms of supreme effort, the four psychic powers (also known as the opponent powers), the four controlling faculties, the five mental powers *(bala),* the seven factors of Enlightenment, and the eight factors of the Eightfold Path.

In this book we honor all these teachings but will confine our discussion mostly to the Noble Eightfold Path and satipaṭṭhāna vipassanā, which contains the essence of the Dhamma. *Sati* means noting and observation; while *upaṭṭhāna* means closely and firmly establishing it on the object. That sense of establishment is the reason why the word is translated into English as "establishment" (often, the word "foundation" is used).

The four types of objects are *kāya,* or material objects—the body sensations; *vedanā,* feelings of pleasantness, unpleasantness, and neutrality; *citta,* or mental objects; and *dhamma,* or sensing, smelling, and general activities. Satipaṭṭhāna is further qualified by the commentators as a far greater than ordinary mindfulness. It must be an extraordinary, sticking mindfulness that is always established on the object.

It is most important that mindfulness stick to the object. To do so, it has to reach it, first, and then stick into it. We call this *okkantitvā pavattati,* "plunging into the target." We can also call it penetrating continuously. Mindfulness must continuously enter into the object. The characteristic *(lakkhaṇa)* of mindfulness is called *apilāpana lakkhaṇa,* non-superficiality. *Pilāpana* means skimming or bobbing or wobbling. Good mindfulness is not like that. It is not like a cork floating down the river, it is more like a stone sinking down into the mud of the riverbed.

In order to sink into the object, mindfulness needs support from other powers. Vitakka, or aim, is a concentration factor, a factor of absorption *(jhāna).* Only when aim is present will the mind and object be aligned. But the mind won't necessarily reach the object without *ātāpa,* "ardent effort." This effort is not casual, slack, or cool but active, warm, and alert. The mind will sink into any object, whether it is the rising and falling, body objects, feelings, or thinking and planning. General activities like seeing will also be covered.

Texts, discourses, and discussions will have established a basic sense of faith and confidence. One must know the benefits of practice to a greater or lesser extent—then one will have greater faith, and make the effort that is necessary to send the mind vigorously toward the object of mindfulness, with such energy that the attention will be able to sink into the object of mindfulness.

The Buddha said, "Monks, this is the certain and sure way for the purification of beings." He meant that satipaṭṭhāna vipassanā can clear up craving, anger, and delusion all the way to arahantship. Trusting in the guidance of the Buddha, believing that the Dhamma is in fact the truth, *saddhā,* "faith" or "confidence," will arise. One will want to confirm the belief that this is true. Then one will have *chanda,* a desire to practice. Once one is practicing, one needs support from aim and effort.

A meditator's mind must continuously enter and penetrate the object. The mind should sink into its object *(pavattati)* at all times. When an object arises the mind has to be with it all the time, second by second, not losing sight of it. This is the function of mindfulness called *asammosa rasa,* meaning non-forgetfulness or keeping the object in view. One must no longer miss or forget the object, and not slip off from it.

The function of mindfulness works like forking up a mouthful of food. If there is only aim, the fork will never stick in, let alone be lifted to the mouth. Effort is also needed, but effort alone is no good either. A combination of factors must be there.

The arising object and the observing mind have to meet face to face. The observation can't arise after the object has departed, or before the object has arrived. There must be a confrontation. This is the manifestation of mindfulness known as *visaya-abimukha bhāva paccupaṭṭhāna,* the quality of being face to face continuously with the object. The defilements have no chance to enter the stream of consciousness. It is also said of mindfulness that it has the quality of *arakkhā paccupaṭṭhāna,* or protecting the mind from defilements.

Thus one gains *vimutti,* freedom from bondage, and also *santi,* peace. There is no more agitation due to lust, anger, and ignorance. When peace arises second by second, it is the basis of happiness. When lust, anger, and delusion continuously enter, there is no freedom and no protection. When the mind is aligned with the rising and falling of the abdomen and with the appearance and predominance, from time to time, of other objects, then one is free from those three types of tormenting thoughts. Effort closes and blocks the path of unwholesomeness.

The proximate condition for the arising of mindfulness is *thirasaññā padaṭṭhāna,* a strong perception, recording, or recognition of objects. Do not choose objects, just record what comes, whether you like it or not. The continuity of *sati* will cause the mind to fall into *avikkhepa samādhi,* "nondistracted concentration." *Uddhacca-kukkucca,* "restlessness and remorse," will disappear. The mind will become stable, settled, no longer agitated and chaotic. As much as mindfulness arises, it will be fixed and stable.

## The Speed of Mindfulness

Early in one's practice, mindfulness has no speed. There is not enough buildup of energetic effort, and so the moments of attention will be intermittent. One will feel that one is barely catching just a few moments' experience. But the mind does gather some speed when it plunges into the object. For those who meditate regularly, the speed of their mindfulness gradually increases over time. But for those whose practice is full of holes and gaps, who like to take little breaks and breathers, there is a need to learn how to sustain continuity.

A meditator who makes an honest, respectful effort to note each arising object will attain concentration and wisdom—provided that his or her mindfulness is also strong in the preceding and succeeding moments. Then, too, he or she will gain the power to note the object automatically. This happens particularly at the time of the fourth insight knowledge (the fourth *ñāṇa*), the insight into the arising and passing away of objects. One sees dramatically the rapidity with which objects arise and pass away.

Between this and the fifth insight knowledge, which focuses on the dissolution of all objects, mindful noting still seems to be moving slower than the objects themselves. This is true for everybody during those stages of practice, no matter how diligently and continuously they are practicing. It is simply part of the unfolding of the insights.

Two strategies can be applied at this time. The first is simply to continue as before, labeling and observing all objects as carefully as possible, noting "rising" and "falling" synchronously with the movements of the abdomen in the sitting meditation; and "lifting," "moving," and "placing" in sync with the movements of the foot in walking meditation.

Alternatively, one can simply be aware without labeling each arising object.

When the noting momentum is very good, mindfulness races to the target. Vitakka and vicāra, aiming and rubbing, the two concentration factors that aim the mind accurately and gather it into the object, will be present. Viriya, or effort, will propel the mindful awareness energetically until it reaches and sticks to the target.

This continuous, forceful momentum is called *pakkhanditvā pavattati,* "continuously rushing." Notice the particle *pa* here. *Pa* has the same meaning as it does in the word *satipaṭṭhāna*—it means "extraordinary." There should be an extraordinary, almost explosive speed to this mindfulness. It should also be *bhusattha,* "excessive, intensive, and persistent." Then mindfulness will not slip off, spread out, or leave.

When effort is of high quality, so is mindfulness. With extraordinary effort, the mind will not slip off the object and higher and higher insights will become available.

In the early phases of practice, the gross hindrances of desire, anger, sleepiness, restlessness, and doubt have to be overcome by an initial determined effort. After that we apply *paggahita viriya,* continuously uplifting effort. This is like lifting an object and then holding it up, without putting it back down on the ground. Then effort will become *paripuṇṇa viriya,* or fulfilled effort.

## *Urgency and Haste*

We are describing extraordinary mindfulness (bhusattha sati). The term for effort is *ātāpa,* which, we said, means "urgent exertion." This word *ātāpa* comes from the Satipaṭṭhāna Sutta, and it connotes a quality of warmth. Effort should not be cool or detached, or else the mind will shrink, congeal, and become inactive as a stick of butter in a refrigerator.

To soften butter you heat it. To make the mind pliable and workable, you apply ātāpa. Hot, burning effort!

Kilesas, especially tiredness and laziness, arise in a cold mind. *Thīna-middha,* the hindrance of sloth and torpor, comes and blocks the path of wholesomeness. Sloth weakens the mind and prevents wisdom from unfolding. To dispel thina-middha, one sharpens the aim of awareness, accurately directing the mindfulness toward the object. This opens and refreshes the mind. Effort is important here as well.

Yogis whose practice is in a shambles are always the ones who are practicing in an easygoing, casual way. These yogis have boring meditations: day in, day out, they experience the same things. Since their mind does not reach the object, they see nothing. Nothing happens, and the progress of insight does not unfold.

Physical activity leads to tiredness. Not so with the mind. When the mind is used a lot, it gets stronger, like a car battery that charges up as the car travels.

Yogis who look around here and there, who sit and think or are not continuous in practice, need to be pushed by their teachers. They need to be told "Aim, focus! Don't let your mind slip off! Please apply effort!" and so forth. When a meditator practices like that, momentum becomes outstanding. If a meditator's practice is diligent, respectful, and consistent, she or he will have top-quality mindfulness.

According to commentators on the Satipaṭṭhāna Sutta, mindfulness should be *pakkhandana,* "hastily speeding" or "hurriedly rushing" toward the object. As soon as an object arises, one hastily notes it. Objects arise right now and they also vanish right now, so one has to use excellent aim and great effort to catch them. No sooner has an object arisen than it disappears! You have to catch up with this rapidity and follow the object as closely as possible. Nothing else matters. There is no time for anything else—certainly not for musing, cogitating, or speculating.

There's no time to ask why, what, or how. If you stop to ask, the mind won't reach the object, missing it and falling into darkness.

If you have *pakkhanditvā pavattati,* continuous rushing toward the object, you have good or perhaps even very good meditation.

### *Capturing the Object by Sudden Attack*

As soon as an object arises the meditator should attack and capture it, in order to know its nature. *Anupassanā,* which means "contemplation"—frequent contemplation—can only succeed by rushing to the object right when it arises with one's mindful awareness. Then wisdom can arise. But if mindfulness is not right there when the object arises, delusion will take over. There will be not only delusion but ahirika and anottappa, lack of shame and lack of fear of wrongdoing. Separating from the object, the noting mind flies off. Restlessness, aversion, agitation, ill will, sloth, and sensuous desire will fill the mind for a longer or shorter period of time.

People who lack mindfulness lose possession of their body and mind. They allow defilements to become the landlord. To repossess your own body and mind, attack the arising objects with instantaneous awareness!

In the texts, the six sense doors are called *bhūmi,* translated as "fields" or "realms" and indicating an area where something arises. The *kilesa bhūmi,* a realm governed by the kilesas, is the inheritance of a weak meditator.

Courage is needed to attack the objects at all six sense doors. Sometimes you lose, sometimes you win. As you become more skilled and successful, wisdom will arise. A respectful, diligent meditator inherits the *paññā bhūmi,* the field of wisdom.

The gist of this is that if one does not observe with energetic mindfulness, the sense doors become a field of defilements. When you habitually miss the object, the kilesa bhūmi arises intermittently.

## The Two Fields

### *The Field of Kilesas*

You are attacking the object day and night, closely attending to moment-by-moment experience at the six doors. Now, insight knowledges will begin to arise for you. If, on the other hand, your mindfulness does not reach the target in time, defilements will emerge instead. Then there will be no knowledge. Ignorance will sit around in both of its ugly forms: simple unknowing and the perverted unknowing that leads into wrong views.

People who do not contemplate objects carefully will be full of wrong views about the nature of life. They are the ignorant inhabitants of the kilesa field. Others will come to know the nature clearly. They will live in the paññā bhūmi, the field of wisdom. In Dhamma terms we could say this is like the difference between living in poverty on a weed-infested vacant lot—renting a hovel from a mean landlord—and enjoying freedom and prosperity, living in your own fine mansion surrounded by lovely gardens of wisdom. Of course, we are not referring to worldly wealth, the amount of money one has in the bank.

The word *bhūmi* literally means virgin soil. It could be a place for trees to grow, for human beings to stand on, for animals to graze, or for inanimate objects to be placed. Objects arising at the six sense doors are considered a field. The eye, ear, nose, tongue, body, and mind are a field. There is no soul involved.

When I speak, it is not because I have a soul that is speaking. There is no ineffable "self" hidden behind my body and mind. It is important to understand that the word *I* is a useful convention, making it simpler to talk about the process of body and mind. If we look closely "I" is a way of discussing the arising of some thoughts, a mental impulse to speak. The sound waves I then produce are called the "striker" element. They hit what is called the "receptor" element, the listener's ear sensitivity. There is no permanent self involved there either. At the moment of contact between the striker and receptor element, hearing will arise.

The experience of hearing consists of three elements: contact *(phassa),* ignition, and feeling *(vedanā).* First comes phassa. For phassa to occur, an ear must be present, there must be a sound, and there must be consciousness. These three elements converge in the moment of contact. Then there is ignition, an experience of hearing. This ignition is a mental experience without a permanent entity involved. Third, there will be some feeling, either of pleasantness, unpleasantness, or neutrality, associated with hearing the sound. The whole thing is a mere process.

If hearing occurs during a gap in mindfulness, moha and avijjā, delusion and ignorance, are produced as well. A big clump of kilesas will jump into the fray. Along with delusion and ignorance, ahirika and anottappa, lack of moral shame and absence of moral fear—which amount to a lack of conscience or inclination to misbehave—will be present. Without mindfulness, there's no concentration, so the mind will also be restless and agitated *(uddhacca).*

The kilesa-weeds thrive in the field of the sense doors. They are growing there at all times except when we are mindful—or asleep. Our life can become a kilesa forest, choked with toxic, ugly weeds. When weeds take over and multiply in a field, it is clearly not beneficial. The field is hideous to look at and may even be dangerous to enter.

People do have the unfortunate capacity to wish harm, torment, and death upon each other, and upon other living beings. If we are not mindful we might indulge such impulses, and incur bodily harm or cause harm to others. In the area of speech, falsehood, backbiting, rough and coarse speech, or useless blabber can arise. Or, we can covet others' property; we can hold and promulgate wrong views, which will lead to further mistakes and misbehavior by ourselves or others. Loading up our lives with harmfulness, foolishness, and uselessness, we sink below the level of a true human being.

Let this be clear: without mindfulness, it is impossible to achieve the insight that makes one a beneficial, superior being.

It's as if we have inherited an overgrown and neglected plot of land. We need to clear away the weeds that have taken over, choking the valuable hardwoods. If we get rid of the invasive weeds, and plant more trees, along with other healing and ecologically appropriate plants, the land will recover its beauty and balance and our property will become valuable.

### *The Field of Wisdom and Purity*

When one comes to know the experience of hearing clearly, for example, one will come to know the three elements of contact, ignition, and feeling. One will understand that all experiences arise in the same way: lawfully, yet without any need for a self or soul.

Mindfulness intervenes, falling on the object. In that moment *khaṇika samādhi,* "momentary concentration," is present. Mindfulness sees clearly that the sound waves are matter, materiality. Or it could also target something else—the ear sensitivity, or the ignition element—with the clear understanding that these, too, are forms of materiality. Or perhaps the hearing consciousness, contact, and feeling will be known and understood to be mere mental events, forms of mentality. More generally, one will come to understand the experience of hearing as simply a convergence of mind and matter, consciousness and sound.

As one becomes aware of all these mental and material events, one will understand the nature of life. This is the first insight, seeing into mind and matter. One is inhabiting the paññā bhūmi, the field of wisdom, adding to the value of one's life.

Meditators who observe the rising and falling of breath at the abdomen will come to see that experience in great detail. They will see that the rising movement consists of a series of segments: it is not one thing. The concepts of "breath," of "rising and falling," and even of "abdomen" will be put into the context of wisdom. The actual nature of life will become clearer.

At the outset meditators must use force to align the mind with objects of experience. Later, during the insight knowledge of arising and passing away, no special effort is required. The mind will feel malleable, agile, workable. Great faith in the practice arises, such that the meditator will try very earnestly to sustain its continuity, feeling a sense of dread and fear lest any gaps be allowed to occur. This is a form of hiri and ottappa, moral shame and moral fear, particular to this phase of practice. The meditator's conscience applies itself to help him or her stay on track. At this time, he or she will also tend to remember past wrongdoings—and, with a new understanding that these arose due to lack of mindfulness, will resolve never to repeat them. As the mind and body feel light and flexible, it often becomes possible to sit for long hours.

The field of experience will be clear and clean. The owner of that field will feel satisfied, just as the owner of a plot of land feels glad to gaze upon a property cleared of weeds and made beautiful by his or her own efforts. But if a gardener doesn't tend his or her plot, weeds take over. Body and mind are like a garden in this sense: if neglected, kilesa-weeds will grow. But if the plot is well tended, it will be beautiful and fruitful.

If you capture the object with outstanding mindfulness, you move into the paññā bhūmi, the realm of wisdom. But if you don't, kilesas thickly sprout and you are trapped, doomed to inhabit the kilesa bhūmi, the realm of the defilements.

Only when one notes and observes the presently arising object will one see its true nature. There is no axiom more basic. Wisdom, paññā, means clear-cut, distinct, discerning, direct knowledge. Dhamma, the true nature of reality, can only be seen at this very moment—in the moment of actually seeing, hearing, touching, tasting, smelling, or thinking. When the abdomen is rising and falling due to the breathing process, when sitting down, when lifting, moving, and placing the foot due to the walking process, when turning around, when eating, when opening the eyes, this is when the true nature of the object can be captured by the attentive awareness.

We must attend to the presently arising object with forceful, urgent, hasty awareness. All activities are included in this one instruction. Mindfulness can, and should, strike only at the objects arising in the present moment. Objects of the past are no more. Objects of the future have not arisen yet. These objects are not present and therefore cannot be ascertained. The Buddha never recommended what is uncertain.

Yogis who get lost in the imagination live in past and future. They can meditate a month or two, even years without any special results. They waste their time.

All presently arising objects need to be noted with full force and accurate aim. Capturing object after object, one's mindfulness becomes excellent. One is able to see clearly and precisely the nature of what is going on.

If one eats with awareness, for example, one comes to know the tastes of all foods clearly and with certainty. There are seven tastes which one will discern clearly: sour, sweet, bitter, spicy, salty, alkaline, and astringent. Furthermore, one will know any and all mental responses that arise in response to the food. Every type of food has a flavor and so do objects of observation.

With direct observation one experiences the body as an interplay of four great elements. These are expressed directly as sensations. Thus, what we experience as hardness, softness, and roughness in the body is the earth element. The water element consists of the sensations of fluidity, flowing, and oozing. The heat element *(tejo-dhātu)* consists of the sensations of hotness, coldness, warmth, and lightness. The air element is movement and support, as well as vibration, piercing, and tension or stiffness. There is no sensation that does not express one of the four elements.

Each of these elements has a specific quality or flavor *(rasa)*. The elements are also called *sabhāva,* meaning that they are presently existing or presently arising. They did not exist in the past, nor will they exist in the future; they exist only in the present moment. They are not mediated by concepts but rather seen by direct awareness in the present.

The Pāḷi term *nāma-rūpa* means "mind (and) body." All presently arising objects of experience are our nāma-rūpa phenomena, our mind and body. We also speak of nāma-rūpa as "mind and matter," or "materiality and mentality." Each member of the mind-matter pair has a particular nature and quality that the meditator must come to know.

When we focus attention on the breathing process at the abdomen, if we have a mental image of the abdomen or hold any type of mental notion of its shape, these are *paññātti,* "concepts." Even the labels "rising" and "falling" do not correspond precisely to sensations: rising and falling are also concepts. One must focus on sensations in and of themselves. Sensations are direct experiences. Concepts are not.

The same goes for having any sense of the mode of the abdomen: say, that it is "inflating" and "deflating." This is *ākāra-paññātti,* a concept that does not represent the true nature or sabhāva, the way of being in the present. Similarly, the beginning, middle, and ending of the rising and falling is not a thing to look for. One must fully note the rising and falling in itself, not isolate some idea about its beginning, middle, or end. When we focus mindfulness directly upon the breathing process at the abdomen, then *sabhāva-rasa,* the flavor of its true nature, will be known directly as experiences of stiffness, hardness, motion, warmth, and other sensations. These all occur here and now, immediately, and without any intervening concepts.

To get to know the true nature we must note and observe the mind-body process directly, at the very moment of its arising. Then we will see *paramattha-dhamma,* or ultimate reality. What can be observed and seen directly, without the intervention of a concept, is paramattha.

At the outset of one's practice, the mind very often falls into a concept, such as the notion of "rising" and "falling." That is okay, and normal, in the beginning. Early on in practice, awareness tends to be more superficial. Special knowledge arises after you can connect the awareness with genuine experiences such as tension, stiffness, or movement in the rising. In turn, these can only be detected while this so-called rising is taking place. The experience of tension is materiality, *rūpa.* Knowledge of the tension is mentality, *nāma.* Knowing either one of these directly is wisdom, *paññā.*

You no longer see mind and matter mixed together, agglutinated;

you discern that they are two. You will see a series of tensions in the so-called rising, and you will also see a series of moments of knowing. To see in this way is wisdom. You have set foot on the path of insight knowledge.

If you see tension, stiffness, and movement in the rising, then your awareness is correct. Bit by bit, as the practice goes on, the mind gets closer and closer to the object. More and more is known; you will see physical and mental experiences in far more detail.

It is analogous to a line of ants crossing the road. A "line of ants" is a concept. "Moving creatures" is still a concept. When we make out individual ants, this is like seeing the true nature. If you want to know the true nature of an object, you have to label and observe it; then you will come to know it in an outstanding way.

Let us take the example of sitting down. Nāma and rūpa are there; sitting down is a series of mental and physical events. Without intention, which is mental, no sitting down would happen. Does the intention to sit down erupt from an individual soul? No. If you are experiencing it directly you will see that there is nothing but a mental process. What about the material events of sitting down—motion, heaviness, contact, and so forth? Do these material events prove the existence of a self? Again, no! If you observe the process of sitting down just as it takes place, a series of intentions and movements is all that you will find. Without this direct observation anyone will assume that "I" am sitting down. This is to take what does not exist, to exist. This is wrong view.

When one respectfully, carefully, diligently, and closely observes sitting down, one will discover a series of mental intentions and physical movements. This is paññā bhūmi. If one does not observe the process closely one will not discover or learn anything. This lands one in kilesa bhūmi. It's as simple as that. Intention is the cause, movement the effect. Without a cause, the movement will never take place. No supreme being nor any concept of a self is involved. The sensations are not a person. Intention too is impersonal, a mere mental event.

Meditators who fail to practice like this will not come to know anything about themselves. They will continue to operate in the realm of arbitrary concepts, faulty assumptions, and wrong views. In one minute, these people will undergo sixty moments of unknowing. In five minutes, they will experience three hundred instances of ignorant confusion. In an hour there are thirty-six hundred seconds during which such people will not be knowing anything. In many hours, there will be a terrific accumulation of confusion, ascribing events to irrelevant causes. The mind will be overgrown, darkened, and entangled with misunderstanding.

If we don't want to live in this way, we can practice *yathābhūta-ñāṇa-dassana,* seeing and knowing in accordance with reality. As the ancient teachers and commentators have already admonished us, the way to accomplish this is simply to note each presently arising object with *pakkhandana sati,* rushing toward the object.

## The Disease and Its Cure

Defilements come in three grades: coarse, medium, and subtle. Coarse *(vītikkama)* kilesas are the transgressive defilements, expressed in physical or verbal action. Medium *(pariyuṭṭhāna)* kilesas are obsessive defilements, gripping and torturing the mind. The subtle or latent defilements *(anusaya kilesa)* lurk under the surface only to burst forth under the right conditions.

The three grades can be compared to a madman who is awake and active, a madman who is just waking up, and a madman who is deeply asleep, literally dormant. The simile of fire is good too: the transgressive kilesas are like a raging forest fire, the obsessive kilesas are like a burning match, and the latent kilesas are like the sulfurous tip of a match—or like the spark from a match that has just been struck. Soon the spark will hit something flammable, though, and the burning will begin.

At birth, the anusaya defilements ride into existence along with us. They arise within the flow of nāma-rūpa, mind and body. As long as they are unchecked, the anusaya kilesas flow in a constant stream. This stream, called *santāna,* arises because the innate, latent defilements have not yet been cut off by insight meditation. Being always present, these innate defilements attach themselves to all of our perceptions. They have the potential to become obsessive or transgressive defilements whenever the right conditions arise: whenever we are not in full control of ourselves or our mental state. We have buttons that can be pushed, which give rise to intense craving and destructive mental patterns.

The santāna stream follows each being, implanted within the stream of consciousness and taken to be an integral part of it. The commentarial texts compare this continuity of defilement to the disease of malaria. The infected person's first bout comes on with a very high fever. This severe attack is like the transgressive defilements. Doctors take steps to lower the fever, which then recurs every two or three days. This is like the obsessive defilements, which afflict the mind intermittently. Finally, the patient begins taking a course of malaria medicine. There is no more fever, but the disease organism remains in the body. This is like the latent defilements. If the patient stops taking the medicine the disease will recur, but if the patient diligently doses himself, the medicine will gradually erode the population of parasites until it utterly vanishes from the body.

Defilements arise from contact at any or all of the six sense doors. When physical and mental objects arise, and one is unmindful, one will not see their nature. All objects are impermanent, unsatisfactory, and uncontrollable. But without awareness one will perceive a solid world full of lasting objects, feelings worth clutching, people to despise or desire. This type of reactivity is also called "object-related kilesas."

If one does not know satipaṭṭhāna vipassanā meditation and is unable to distinguish clearly between mind and matter, the mind slips away from seeing the truth. Instead it will construct, and attempt to rely upon, the notion of an abiding self. This means it will misperceive inner and outer objects as if they were truly solid and permanent—a delusion. When there is no mindfulness, latent defilements attach themselves to objects, creating a continuous stream of confusion, and bringing us into conflict with the way things really are. Not only do the latent defilements becloud and bewilder the mind, a form of suffering in itself; they also tend to flare up into full-blown obsessive attacks. The obsessive kilesas create internal pressure toward transgressive action. Transgressions bring forth consequences. By the time the whole chain reaction runs its course, a life, or several lives, can be in ruins.

If, on the other hand, a meditator contemplates each presently arising object, aiming and aligning the mind with it, her or his awareness falls onto the object and sticks to it. Then the object is seen clearly as it is: fleeting, incapable of bringing lasting peace or lasting trouble. In the moment of contemplating an object in this way, one feels it may not be necessary to take action after all. The object goes away on its own. Meanwhile, the anusaya kilesas have been temporarily cut off, reactivity does not arise, and the peace of an independent mind begins to be felt. There is a chain reaction but in the other direction, the direction of wholesomeness.

When practicing satipaṭṭhāna vipassanā meditation, if the observation of objects is casual and superficial, the mind becomes like a cow ruminating the grass it has eaten throughout the day. Some meditators can sit and ruminate for a very, very long time about objects they experienced in the past. This is a good sign that kilesas are present! Such meditators hoard up defilements to go over them again and again. However, if the observation of objects is ardent and focused, there is no rumination, no hoarding of positive or negative past events. One simply stays with the arising object.

Then the practice is more like taking a photograph. Light reflected from the external object has the chance to reach the film.

To avoid storing up kilesas, you must note the arising object right away. A thousand times it must be said—mindfulness has to reach the object first, before the defilements have a chance! Meditators who are not well grounded in morality, who let their minds roam, who don't note the object with respect for the importance of the meditation practice they are doing, will be plagued with defilements. New meditators are said to be thick with defilements. This is because they are not really familiar with the method of practice. In time, with sincerity, they will learn to perform the instructions. Everyone has been a beginner at some point, even the arahants.

### *Diseases of the Mind*

Worldly, unenlightened beings in general are covered with defilements. They cope with madness and burning of many kinds. Acting on greed, they suffer the madness of greed. Acting on hate, they suffer the madness of hate. Acting on delusion, they suffer the madness of delusion. In addition to all this, they suffer the madness of grief and wrong views, such as the notion of permanence. All of these are the diseases of the mind, *mānasikaroga.*

The Dhamma Vinaya is the method given by the Buddha to cut off all of these painful mental illnesses. If we apply Dhamma Vinaya to our lives, our afflictions will be cured. But it is not easy.

Some malaria patients spit out their medicine. Or they throw down the plate of recommended food and leave the hospital. Insight meditation, satipaṭṭhāna vipassanā, is a demanding practice. You note the object once or twice and then suddenly your mind wanders off. It happens to everyone. If you don't bring the mind back to the presently arising object right away, that's like spitting out the medicine. Some meditators don't have enough faith in the method of practice and give up. That is like throwing away the plate of food. The food and medicine of satipaṭṭhāna vipassanā don't go down so easily. A teacher has to be patient until the meditation fully enters the person and fills their body and mind. Meditators, too, must be patient and courageous.

When one takes medicine and nutritious food, new materiality forms in the body. Similarly, satipaṭṭhāna vipassanā meditation can give rise to amazing developments uplifting the mind to a degree that one might be tempted to exclaim, "Wow, the world looks really different to me. Before I practiced meditation, I would never have imagined such ease of mind was available!" This is due to the power of the mental factors of faith, effort, mindfulness, concentration, and wisdom which are developed by the practice.

The Buddha was the great physician. He has given us the medicine. Like an expert pharmacist, he concocted the training, combining morality, concentration, and wisdom into a powerful healing brew. Like a conscientious researcher, he first tested the medicine on himself. Finding it safe and effective, he examined the world with his omniscience and saw that others, too, could use it. At that point he began distributing his prescription widely.

There does exist a community of people in whom these defilements have been appeased. At the stage of nonreturner, the third stage of enlightenment, there is no more greed and hatred. If you try to imagine this state, you will no doubt find it a worthwhile goal to strive for. Don't assume it's beyond your capacity! The Buddha intended the medicine for you.

### *Healing the Mind and World*

Human beings go to doctors when they are struck by physical diseases. But ordinary physicians cannot cure our most profound, existential maladies; the Buddha has taken responsibility for these. His threefold training is powerful enough to cut off all of the kilesas that make us suffer. We could call meditation practice "medication" practice! For medication practice, we first establish a healthy, balanced lifestyle of morality. This foundation allows us to take the powerful "drugs" of concentration and wisdom that will kill the germs inside us. These are potent medicines, but we apply them according to the Buddha's instructions; and we know we can trust them because he first experimented on himself. Then he tried his techniques on a control group: his first disciples. Their liberation is recorded in the suttas.

Nowadays the Saṅgha, the holy assembly of practitioners, remains engaged in taking the medicine. We are suppressing the hindrances, moving toward a cure for the afflictions by using Dhamma Vinaya. Over the past few thousand years many people have healed and even cured themselves of suffering.

The mind of a practitioner becomes calm and refined. With stream entry, all apāya-related defilements are cut off. There are no more defilements strong enough to lead us into states of loss. A stream-enterer no longer feels the urge to transgress any of the five precepts. He or she also has a basic understanding that the Buddha, Dhamma, and Saṅgha are reliable refuges.

The kilesas must be dispelled! It is a huge relief to know this can, in fact, be done. If you have not yet experienced path and fruition knowledges, imagine the relief in your mind when it is freed from the kilesas' influence. If you have experienced at least one path and fruition stage, consider the further possibilities. Would you enjoy being completely cooled, at peace?

### *How to Take the Buddha's Medicine*

You can certainly regain your health by taking Dhamma medicine, especially if you note the following important points:

You must listen to the physician's instructions.
You must apply meditation regularly.
You must apply meditation effectively, not stopping and starting.
You must complete the course of treatment.

Neither Buddha, Dhamma, nor Saṅgha can help a meditator who isn't willing to listen to the instructions and put them into practice for himself or herself. Changing doctors all the time doesn't lead to a cure either. You will simply become a chronic patient.

Taking only part of the medicine is almost worse than not taking it at all. If you follow only one of the recommendations and ignore the rest, it's like swallowing a prescription capsule without, for example, eating the nutritious food that should go along with it. The medication can damage your stomach lining, making you sicker than before. Taking morality lightly while considering oneself to be a powerful meditator, for example, makes it extremely difficult to cure the diseases of the mind.

Morality is like the mouth of practice. The mouth can provide the body with food only if it can open wide enough and is intact, free of sores and cankers. Morality too must be big enough, and not impaired, in order to nourish the mind with concentration and wisdom.

If you fulfill the three trainings and attain stream entry, you'll be free of belief in a soul, or any essential enduring basis for a self. You'll see that all beings consist of mind and matter, just a stream of effects flowing from causes. You'll be free from wavering and doubt about the Dhamma teachings, for you'll understand how they connect to the nature of reality. Your mind will become lighter and no longer experience the same burning, tormenting urges as before. This security is well worth having.

## How to Disentangle Yourself through Wisdom

In satipaṭṭhāna vipassanā meditation, discoveries are never made by pondering, reading, or discussion. The only way to understand the nature of mind and body, nāma-rūpa, is to observe objects at the six sense doors with direct awareness.

By observing mentality and materiality correctly, knowledge and vision arise such that one clearly understands that there is no individual soul, but rather only a stream of mental and physical events. When one is not observing the presently arising objects at the six sense doors, there will be no clear seeing and therefore no knowledge. People who have never received the instructions to observe their experience directly will tend not to look at these processes directly when they arise. Therefore they will never experience things according to reality but instead take what they see as a composite. This erroneous perception is called *saññā-vipallāsa.*

Thus, if they are in the process of sitting down, people will tend to misperceive the process and think, "*I* am sitting down" or "There is a man (or a woman) sitting down." This repeated misperception is the cause of clinging to a self.

It happens especially in the case of the mind. Mental events are almost invariably construed as designating a self. Indeed, the process of experience at all the sense doors—seeing, hearing, smelling, tasting, touching, and thinking—just gets lumped together and is taken as a whole, a composite consciousness. This composite is assumed to be a person, to be "owned" by someone. To observe the mind-body process in this mistaken fashion, seeing a person instead of the mere arising of mind and matter, is known as *diṭṭhi-vipallāsa,* the perversion of view.

Not being able to see presently arising objects as they truly exist is called *avibhūta.* Avibhūta is the basis for the wrong view that clings to a composite and interprets it as a self, soul, person, or individual.

In reality, the mind initiates activities. There is an impulse and then activities arise. People also take the mind to be continuous when in fact it is constantly changing. It is arising and passing away. People who believe in a soul or personal essence even think that consciousness remains alive after the body breaks up.

Only direct, mindful awareness can finally prove the truth to anyone. However, in order to be free of a belief in self or soul, beginning meditators also need to hear some theoretical explanations. Discussions, explanations, discourses, and interviews offer a preliminary, basic theoretical understanding. The meditator can then go forth and confirm, in practice, that the idea of a self or soul does not correspond to reality.

A teacher must first explain what the student will see and later substantiate the student's reports. Very often, meditators are surprised by this insight about nonself, which reverses the habitual pattern; it tends to be accompanied by a feeling of relief. For example, in sitting down, there is not just one initial intention but a series of intentions, each one followed by material events. The whole process of material and mental events occurs as an interconnected series. Not seeing a self isn't painful; it is joyous, as if one were relieved of a burden.

At the beginning of meditation practice, you get to know the body, or rūpa, by becoming aware of the obvious physical sensations. As mindfulness grows more powerful, you will be able to discern nāma, or mind—in this case, intention. You will see that an intention is one thing, and physical events another. Thus, you can distinguish mind from matter instead of lumping them into one glob.

This is called *nāma-rūpa-yathā-bhūta-ñāṇa-dassana,* "seeing mind and body according to reality." When you are able to see in this way, you spontaneously understand that a mental intention does not constitute a self or soul, nor does the overall process contain or constitute a self or soul. It is not the soul or self who sits down; it is a mere process happening. Maybe the thought "I'm sitting down" will crop up somewhere along the line; yet this does not interfere with the insight: the thought is seen as a mere mental phenomenon, slated for a natural demolition. In other words, while perceiving the overall process of mind and body with continuous mindfulness, it becomes obvious that the "I" thought is an impermanent, fleeting mental object. It lacks the extraordinary, undeserved distinctions attributed to it out of ignorance, avibhūta, not seeing clearly.

In order to gain this knowledge one must approach a teacher. A person who hears these instructions and then practices them will eventually come to a direct decision. "Yes, this is correct. There is only materiality and mentality." This is a vipassanā axiom.

As a meditator gains knowledge, faith and confidence also arise. Progressing through the insight knowledges, weak knowledge and confidence develop into strong understanding and faith. Seeing the mind as one thing and matter as another becomes a comprehensive understanding that applies to all activities of past and future and is valid for everyone.

The mind-body process is called *sa-kāya,* distinct aggregates of materiality and mentality. (The prefix *sa-* means distinct; *kāya* means aggregate.) This is its actual nature, as will be seen by one who observes clearly. But if there's no clear seeing these aggregates will be perceived as a composite, glued together with *atta-diṭṭhi,* self-view. *Sa-kāya-diṭṭhi,* the view that sees nothing more than distinct mind and matter, is not a mere Buddhist doctrine; rather, it is a direct perception, born of a direct examination.

Making the transition away from wrongful self-view is the form of purification called *diṭṭhi-visuddhi,* or purification of view. This means that the idea that mind and matter are permanent in themselves, and also that they are somehow signs of a permanent, independently existing self, is removed. The self is seen to be imaginary. If we don't observe carefully, without exception all of us will assume a self or soul is there—even Buddhists.

## No Person behind the Process

The term *puthujjana,* "worldling," refers to a person who has not yet experienced stream entry. Such people do not see reality, or mind and matter, as it is. Instead, a view forms of a being or personality. They assume a central self is at the controls of their experience. This is a wrongful belief that brings much pain and frustration.

*Yathā-bhūtā* means to be in accord with reality. When seeing according to reality, one sees that a relevant cause is linked to the relevant effect. Life in its totality is just a continuum of cause-and-effect relations. While one can see the operation of cause and effect, one can act in harmony with the way things really are. If one's assumptions are misguided, one's responses will be the same.

The sitting-down or standing-up process is a mere flow of materiality and mentality. If there is no intention, there will never be a process. Due to one mental phenomenon, another arises. For example, if the eye is not turned toward a visual object, or even if it is and the attention is elsewhere, no seeing will occur. The mind must touch the object. While observing the rising and falling of the abdomen, if you aren't observing any other objects, you will not notice or come to know them. Attention *(manasikāra)* is the rudder of the mind. If there is no attention directing the mind toward an object, the object will never be known.

Sometimes a physical object is the cause and a mental object is the effect. If a physical object is present, one can know it. Consciousness or knowing, then, is the mental event that arises as a result of the physical object. Conversely if there's no object present, there is no knowledge. For example, during practice the rising and falling movement can become so subtle as to be imperceptible. Then there is no consciousness of them. Without a cause there is no effect.

Physical objects can also be the causes of other physical objects. For example, when we touch a cold item, a physical reaction occurs. Winter's cold weather leads to the skin's drying out and cracking. Summer's heat leads to sweating and exhaustion. Hunger brings weakness and eventually the withering of the body. With intake of material food, the body is refreshed and nourished. All of these are physical effects of physical causes.

Cause and effect must be linked by relevance. Only a relevant cause leads to a relevant effect.

If one is not observing according to reality, *yathā-bhūtā,* delusion will arise. This takes the form of obscurity and indecision. *Sammoha,* delusion, gets very thick in ordinary beings. When there is no observation, the idea of an individual soul or self *(jīva-atta)* will arise. The belief in the existence of a supreme being or spirit *(parama-atta)* can also appear, and along with it the worship of that imaginary being.

Some people believe in fate, that things are totally predetermined; others in accident, that events can happen for no reason. Still other people ascribe fictitious or hypothetical causes to events, such as believing that the parama-atta is doing it all. These are all forms of wrong view. To believe things happen solely due to the kamma from previous existences is also insufficient. That form of incorrect view is called *pubbekata hetuka diṭṭhi.* In reality, consciousness, temperature, or climate and nutriment also contribute to events and experiences.

Seeing cause and effect with knowledge *(ñāṇa-dassana),* one knows the truth for oneself, not because of being told. In the stage of insight where cause and effect become clear, the insight of yathā-bhūtā-ñāṇa-dassana, all doubt is removed. Cause and effect are seen in the present; yet their mechanism is recognized as being valid for all past and future moments.

A supreme being can't enter the picture. Yathā-bhūtā-ñāṇa-dassana also dispels *sammoha-abhinivesa,* or adherence due to thick delusion, bewilderment, and obscurity. It has the quality of completeness, such that one sees there is nothing happening other than this—no jīva-atta, no individual soul; and no parama-atta, no supreme being, either. Discerning cause and effect is *paccaya pariggaha ñāṇa dassana:* very clear and conspicuous, directly evident, and distinct knowledge. It is difficult to overstate the clarity with which this particular insight strikes the mind.

Ignorance, craving, and clinging—*avijjā, taṇhā,* and *upādāna*—are the causes of this existence and of all previous existences. They will also cause future existences unless meditators take care of them right here and now, in this life. At this stage of meditation, the practitioner will feel that the cause of action *(kamma)* lies in ignorance, craving, and clinging, and that the same will hold true in the future.

One can come to a firm and certain decision about many issues—whether or not there is God, why things happen or don't, and why we cannot necessarily control the outcomes of events. This insight dispels wrong beliefs and wrong knowing. There will no longer be any confusion in these areas.

## The Cycles of Saṃsāra

Saṃsāra is a whirl of suffering and affliction. One defilement leads to another in an overall atmosphere of confusion. However, clear analysis reveals saṃsāra to be structured into three interlocking *vaṭṭa,* or cycles. They are related as a chain of causes and effects. The first cycle is *kilesa vaṭṭa,* the cycle of defilement or affliction, which consists of ignorance, craving, and clinging. It also forms the basis or cause for the second cycle, *kamma vaṭṭa. Kamma* means volitional actions, which can be wholesome, unwholesome, or neutral. These actions then lead to results, *vipāka vaṭṭa,* which occur in various ways, some immediate and others more distant. Vipāka vaṭṭa is the third cycle of saṃsāra.

Normally these three vaṭṭas are rotating all the time. To understand how they function, we will use several analogies, starting with the image of a tree.

### *The Case of the Sapling*

Any tree's lifeblood is its juicy, nourishing sap. Sap permeates the tree and drives it to bear fruit, which duly ripens and falls to the ground where it releases seeds. New saplings spring up; when they mature they too bear fruit, sweet or sour depending on the nature of the seeds. But if a sapling does not receive support from the air, water, soil, wind, and sun, it will dry up and no longer propagate its species.

Kilesas are said to be moist, humid, and sticky, rather like sap. In this analogy kilesa vaṭṭa, the cycle of defilement, is the tree sap. Kamma vaṭṭa, the cycle of actions, is the fruit. Vipāka vaṭṭa, the cycle of results, is a new generation of saplings springing up from the seeds. At this point the analogy is particularly apt, given that vipāka vaṭṭa includes *paṭisandhi,* or rebirth into a new existence. From each new birth, as long as the kilesas remain alive, there will be kammic fruits, and these will give rise to many further generations of vipāka.

As for the climate that nurtures the tree, the sensual pleasures of the human, deva, and brahma worlds keep the sap of defilement flowing.

Of the three vaṭṭas, kilesa vaṭṭa is the most important, for it is the cause of the other two. Anytime you remove a cause, its results are automatically taken care of. Dry up kilesa vaṭṭa, then, and there will be no more kamma, no more results: no more rebirth.

*Payoga* is the word for activities like satipaṭṭhāna vipassanā meditation that destroy the defilements. Vipassanā practice breaks the link between pleasant, unpleasant, and neutral experiences and the arising of the related kilesas. Right at the moment when reactivity usually begins, mindfulness intervenes instead. That is why it is so important, in this practice, to make sure one's mindfulness keeps pace with the arising objects.

If a tree is no longer able to get support from the climate, it withers and dies. Anyone who has seen directly into his or her own mind will find it easy to comprehend this linkage.

### *Ignorance Is the Basis for Affliction*

We have seen that the kilesas are the cause of kamma and rebirth. Ignorance, craving, and clinging are the three basic kilesas that make up kilesa vaṭṭa. Of these, avijjā, ignorance, is the most important. It is the cause of all the others; without it they would not arise, so it is crucial to attack ignorance. As the originator of the rest of the kilesas, ignorance is not only responsible for the whole kilesa vaṭṭa but for kamma vaṭṭa and vipāka vaṭṭa to boot.

Though *avijjā* basically means not knowing, in this context it means specifically not knowing the Four Noble Truths. Ignorance of the Four Noble Truths is what keeps saṃsāra going.

Without comprehending the Four Noble Truths, when an object arises one takes an interest in it—in other words, craves it. Next, the mind will attempt to cling to it. This is based on wrong view, the automatic, barely conscious assumption that each and every object possesses permanence and can bring us happiness. Then, of course, the object passes away and we are left in the dust. Wrong views play a huge role in solidifying clinging, which in turn drives mistaken kammic actions that perpetuate suffering for oneself and others.

Ignorance has to be cut off! There is hardly a point more important than this.

### *Off with the Head!*

In the Buddha's time there lived a young hermit. His teacher wanted to know whether the Buddha was really a buddha or not. Being old, the teacher sent the young hermit to one of the Buddha's talks, where he would ask two questions silently, in his mind: "What is the head? How to cut off the head?" The import of these cryptic queries may have been obscure, yet the young hermit duly obeyed.

The Buddha interrupted his discourse and said, "The head is ignorance, not knowing. Vijjā, knowledge, cuts it off—knowledge of the Four Noble Truths. Of these, the Fourth has to be developed. With this knowledge, one gains freedom from ignorance."

Ignorance is called the head of suffering because it sustains all of its cycles, just as the head contains the brain and most of the sense organs. Cutting off a person's head equals death for the body as well as the head itself. Cutting off ignorance, too, puts an end to all aspects of suffering.

The question arises, is knowledge the only thing needed to cut off ignorance? The Buddha's concise answer already addressed this point. He said that the Fourth Noble Truth must be developed. The Fourth Noble Truth is the Noble Eightfold Path. We have discussed how satipaṭṭhāna vipassanā meditation develops all the Noble Path factors.

Indeed, just as the three vaṭṭas follow a cause-and-effect sequence, the arising of knowledge is also the result of causes and effects. Unfortunately, vijjā does not tend to arise by itself. Even the Buddha had to exert very strenuous effort. He left us the Dhamma Vinaya so that we might replicate his results. If we do nothing and merely continue to live in an unwholesome, inattentive way, the three vaṭṭas will continue to whirl. There will be no cause for the arising of insight, nor for the destruction of ignorance.

### *Factors to Develop Knowledge*

When one is engaged in the practice of satipaṭṭhāna vipassanā meditation, insight knowledge develops based on five factors.

1. *Saddhā:* faith and confidence
2. *Chanda:* desire to practice
3. *Viriya:* the effort and courage to observe what should be observed, and refrain from what should be abandoned
4. *Sati:* mindfulness
5. *Samādhi:* concentration and focus

When all these five are present, vijjā, or knowledge, can grow strong enough to cut off the defilements.

Avijjā is the cause of all suffering in saṃsāra, even the cycle of birth and death. Vijjā cuts off ignorance and thereby brings an end to every form of stress that we experience. But this vijjā is not the kind of knowledge we can gain by reading books. We cannot ponder our way to the end of avijjā, nor analyze, discuss, and listen it away. Explanations have their place, as we've mentioned; but eventually we must generate bhāvanā knowledge, meditative insight—the clear seeing which can only happen when the attentive mind falls on an object directly and accurately.

Accuracy is one aspect of samādhi, concentration. Samādhi is the basis and immediate precursor of bhāvanā knowledge. Only when momentary concentration, khaṇika samādhi, is present can bhāvanā knowledge arise instead of ignorance.

Samādhi doesn't arise by itself. Sustained mindfulness is required. In turn, to sustain mindfulness, tremendous effort, viriya, is needed. Viriya is the energy that directs the mind toward the object, impels it all the way, and holds it there until the object has been well seen.

Viriya also has another aspect, that of courage. Mental development is not an easy task. There are inner and outer difficulties along the way; it takes strength to turn away from what is unwholesome and resolve to do whatever it takes to develop wholesomeness.

Courageous effort will not be made without a burning desire *(chanda)* to gain insight knowledge. One might also yearn to experience the benefits of satipaṭṭhāna vipassanā meditation. Since one has not yet experienced the benefits for oneself, one must feel some degree of faith or confidence *(saddhā)*. One must believe the benefits exist and that one can attain them.

Thus saddhā is the first thing needed for the development of knowledge. A student has to feel some faith in the teachings. One must decide, "This is correct." Based on this faith, and desiring the benefits, one goes to a retreat center. There one makes the necessary effort. As a result of this effort, mindfulness arises. The mind falls on the object: concentration is developing. Now, insight knowledge can arise.

Some meditators will reach the direct insights into mind and matter and into cause and effect. Later they may progress to the point where they see directly into the impermanence of all things.

Each person will gain knowledge according to his or her effort. When light comes, darkness is dispelled. This is automatic, natural, definitive.

All of the cause-and-effect links that arise in the body are ultimately *dukkha-sacca,* the Noble Truth of Suffering. You see it by practicing satipaṭṭhāna vipassanā; and along with seeing it, the mind automatically lets go. If you don't practice, you will simply continue to take physical processes as good and beneficial, a potential source of happiness. You'll crave more seeing, hearing, touching, tasting, and thinking. Whatever arises will be clung to. But since objects are not inherently satisfying, there will only be more thirst and frustration.

When the nature of sense processes is clearly seen, one recognizes their inherent danger and limitations. These things are fleeting, unsatisfying, and not subject to anyone's control. Ignorance about them has been severed, so craving and clinging won't arise. Nor will kamma and results. This is what is meant by cutting off the three vaṭṭas. What a relief!

## *The Origin of Craving and Clinging*

The sap in a tree must be supported by the surrounding climate or else the tree will die. The defilements, similarly, need support from the wet, sensuous pleasures of the human realm. Enticing sights, sweet sounds, tasty flavors, soft touches, lofty thoughts—ordinary people desire all of these. Clinging and delusion accumulate around these pleasurable experiences.

Let's be honest. To crave the happiness derived from sense pleasures just means one craves pleasure. This is rather crude. Yet because of ignorance, one assumes that no better form of happiness is available. Alas, in the realm of the senses, we are trapped. There is no experience that does not fade away, leaving us closer to death. To rid oneself of ignorance about sense pleasures is the best thing anyone can do for himself or herself. In truth they're very dangerous.

When the power to note and observe gains force, the meditator will see the rapid arising and passing away of objects. With this stage of insight comes a special Dhamma pleasure. Those who have tasted it agree: it is much better than mere sense pleasure.

We will describe some stages of insight in order to encourage meditators and to give some sense of the lawful unfolding of the practice. But here is an important word of warning: it is not helpful to analyze one's own practice and try to decide what stage of insight one has reached. This is the job of a qualified teacher, one who understands the method. A meditator practicing intensively has only one thing to remember. When there is no mindfulness, ignorance arises. Never let go of mindfulness!

## The Noble Eightfold Path and Where It Leads

No beginning can be found to ignorance, but it definitely can be brought to an end. According to the Buddha's instructions, the Noble Eightfold Path is the method to be developed for this purpose. The path is the cause; vijjā, knowledge, is the effect.

What would it mean to cut off ignorance, the head of saṃsāra, the root of all affliction? This is a question each of us should contemplate and take to heart. When we consider the benefits of meditation practice, we generate faith. Not yet having all of the benefits for ourselves, we will desire to practice further. Strong faith and desire for accomplishment will lead to strong effort; and strong effort will be necessary to accomplish the goal.

In order to develop the Noble Eightfold Path, one's initial effort should be directed into the arena of sīla, or morality. By making a fundamental resolve to uphold and not to violate the morality aspects of the Path—Right Action, Right Speech, and Right Livelihood—wholesome volition arises. The transgressive defilements will begin to be suppressed as well.

A strong intent to uphold sīla is far more effective and potent than some vague notion that one can restrain oneself naturally. Natural restraint is perfected only at the arahant stage. Until then, morality is an area where vigilance and effort are appropriate.

Since Right Intention is part of the wisdom group of the Noble Eightfold Path, we can see how the practice of sīla supports the growth of wisdom. Yet moral vigilance alone cannot cut off ignorance, nor bring about even one stage of insight knowledge, let alone path and fruition consciousness. Having begun to develop wholesome intentions through morality, we must also direct effort into the arena of formal meditation practice. This will help us fulfill the remaining trainings of concentration and wisdom, further aspects of the Noble Eightfold Path. We continue to apply Vinaya discipline as well as entering the Dhamma aspect of Dhamma Vinaya.

The concentration group of the Eightfold Path consists of Right Effort, Right Mindfulness, and Right Concentration. With effort we generate mindfulness toward objects at the six sense doors, labeling and observing them as and when they arise. This precise awareness develops vitakka, the aiming aspect of concentration. Vitakka is in play every time we align the mind with the rising and falling movement of the abdomen, or direct it toward other arising objects. Vitakka naturally leads to vicāra, the rubbing aspect of concentration. Vicāra is what sustains attention on the object until it has been seen, contemplated. With strong vicāra, the meditator is freed from *kāma-cchanda,* "sensual desire," and the other hindrances that prevent wholesomeness from arising. These kilesas are blocked off. This is how the concentration group of the Noble Eightfold Path works to hold back the pariyuṭṭhāna kilesas, the obsessive afflictions.

The mind becomes clear and stable. Agitation disappears. In a calm, clear, concentrated mind *pīti,* "joyful interest," will become strong. Right Aim and Right View, the mental factors of the wisdom group of the Noble Eightfold Path, will be present.

Right View arises when clearly knowing objects at all six sense doors. It is a result of khaṇika samādhi, the mind falling directly onto the object moment after moment. In order to attain this continuous, moment-by-moment concentration, one needs an urgent and continuous exertion of effort.

It is useful for meditators to note that continuous observation, effort, and concentration are the most important elements they must apply in their practice. These are the way to develop all of the factors of the Noble Eightfold Path, culminating in vijjā, or knowledge, which is another way of referring to Right View.

By noting and knowing with diligence, one comes to know the nature of the object. Light arises, darkness is dispelled. The arising of knowledge is equivalent to the destruction of ignorance, cutting off the head of saṃsāra. With every noting and knowing, the relevant parts of the Noble Eightfold Path arise to dispel the defilements. Thus, strengthening and fulfilling all three groups of the path, one gains purity.

One comes to know purely and nobly on the forerunner path, *pubbe-bhāga-magga.* The forerunner path means all of the efforts we put into our practice of Dhamma Vinaya, creating the momentum and conditions for vimutti to arise. When the pubbe-bhāga-magga is fulfilled, one gains freedom from bondage. The complete path includes both effort and fruition in the areas of pure and noble morality, pure and noble concentration, pure and noble wisdom, and finally pure and noble vimutti, or liberation.

### *Noticing Resultants Destroys the Causes*

Dhamma experience also abides by the laws of cause and effect. All of the Noble Path factors belong in the realm of results, vipāka. Faith, desire, and effort are the cause for their arising. Later on, mindfulness and concentration become the cause for the arising of wisdom or

Right View. Again, fulfilling the forerunner aspect of the Eightfold Path is the direct cause of vimutti.

When paṭisandhi citta, rebirth-linking consciousness, arises, kammic potential is passed on from the old to the new existence. Cetasikas, mental factors, and consciousness cause the new being's six sense bases. Our sense doors, then, are the effects of kamma. Thus, the objects to be observed in meditation practice are also part of the realm of vipāka, the results of kamma. If one does not know their nature, kilesa vaṭṭa will arise again and again lead us through the experiences of kamma and vipāka. But by observing resultants, the cause is destroyed, and the cycle of saṃsāra is not perpetuated.

If there is not enough kilesa "sap" or "juice" to form the basis for a new human being, rebirth-linking consciousness will not arise. If we want to cut off that humidity, and avoid getting stuck in the round of endless rebirths, the solution is amazingly simple. All one needs to do is observe the arising object. If we read the text of the Satipaṭṭhāna Sutta, we might feel overwhelmed by the list of things to pay attention to—physical objects, feelings of pleasantness, unpleasantness, and neutrality, mental objects, consciousness, as well as the events at the six sense doors. Once again, however, all of these bases of observation can be summed up in a single instruction: observe all distinctly arising objects. We have already discussed how all factors of the Noble Eightfold Path are present in one moment of noting, including morality and concentration, so we will not repeat that here.

The mind moves toward its object forcefully, urgently. One may feel that one is pushing the attention toward its goal. This movement should be urgent—no attention should be paid to other objects or the surrounding area. *Bhūta,* the existing object, has to be fully grasped and covered. Intense observation such as this deserves the name of satipaṭṭhāna.

## *Observing*

Bhūta are things in existence. Mentality bhūtā, as well as rūpa or bodily bhūtā, are arising and passing away rapidly in a cause-and-effect sequence. The old gives rise to the new. Objects arise and pass away extremely rapidly. They must be quickly and hastily observed. After some time it is no longer necessary to make quite so much effort, since the mind is automatically aligned.

The following verse says it all:

Without the practice of the Eightfold Path
The cycle will spin forever.
The practice of the Eightfold Path
Cuts off the cycle.

When one is not observing, the Eightfold Path cannot be developed. By not developing satipaṭṭhāna vipassanā meditation, beings will slip or err, whether they are laypeople or monastics. If one has slipped, one will not develop the path factors that cause the mind to be noble. Nor will one discover the special meaning of the Noble Path, which is nothing less than path and fruition consciousness, equivalent to nibbāna and vimutti. The cycle of kilesas will begin again because it has not been cut off. One will be impure, ignoble, susceptible to all sorts of immorality.

These are the guidelines for happiness and prosperity laid down by the Buddha. This is the Dhamma. If one stays within its boundary, one has fulfilled the Vinaya discipline. The term *Dhamma Vinaya* is equivalent to *sāsana,* the teaching. If one practices Dhamma Vinaya, one has established the teaching in oneself and thus spreads it.

When one observes the distinctly arising objects with full force, one will come to know their nature. Avijjā cannot arise; it is thus exhausted. To the extent that vijjā arises, avijjā does not. The kilesas dry up. Since no unwholesome acts are performed, no unwholesome results will follow, and no new seeds will form. We see the end of the cycle of action. If one practices according to the instructions, one will perfect the *sammā-dukkha-khaya-gami,* the path that takes one to the complete exhaustion of unsatisfactoriness. And we are still talking only about the forerunner path, the pubbe-bhāga-magga.

## *A Blissful Time in Practice*

With ongoing practice, after the insight into the three characteristics of all objects, meditators can experience *udayabbaya-ñāṇa,* or insight into rising and passing away. As quickly as an object appears, it disappears again. One sees everything in clear and minute detail, with very little effort. The mind is very clear; there are no hindrances; sati is strong and bright and pure. One may see lights and be filled with a sense of joy, rapture, and well-being. There will be a strong mental coolness, a special meditative flavor. One will think, "The Dhamma is good!" With sharp, clear-cut knowledge, the mind sticks to the object. One may have memories of events long past and buried.

The mental environment being extremely pleasant, a subtle attachment to that pleasantness, *nikanti,* also tends to arise at this stage. This nikanti is in fact a refined form of *taṇhā,* or thirst. At the same time, there are many positive qualities to be attached to. Faith arises and frees one from skeptical doubt. Experiencing the mind as clean and beautiful and bright, one feels intensely grateful for the practice, and free from *pamāda,* or negligence. Indeed, one tends to increase the intensity of practice out of a fear of distraction and a sense of shame over one's past lapses. A strong moral feeling will arise in the mind, to the effect that more effort is going to be needed in order to reach liberation. Nongreed and nonhatred, especially toward outward objects, arise at this time. The mind experiences peace and neutral balance, *tatra-majjhattatā.* One will be able to sit easily for one to two hours without pain, because there is such lightness in the body. The mind feels fresh and light, adaptable and lithe, full of energy. A sense of rectitude will arise; one reflects on past misdeeds and resolves not to repeat them.

Dhamma happiness and the delight of practice are far better than worldly delight. At this time one knows this and therefore tends not to think quite so highly of sense pleasures. At this stage, if the meditator can cut through the attachment to internal states such as that pesky nikanti mentioned above, he or she will be able to progress into the higher insight knowledges that still remain, up to the point of realizing the coolness of nibbāna—*sotāpatti magga* and *phala,* the path and fruition of stream entry.

At that point, it will become blindingly obvious that the Dhamma leads to happiness and prosperity. One finally understands what the Buddha intended. Dhamma Vinaya is established in oneself; one will clearly understand, see, and experience the nature of the Buddha's virtues.

## Walking the Path Hand in Hand

In this world there are two kinds of rare and precious beings, difficult to find. These are *upakārī,* or benefactors, and *kataññū,* those who return gratitude for what they have received. Among all benefactors, the Buddha is supreme. He practiced the cause, attained the result, then worked for the benefit of all beings. He is our most rare and valuable benefactor, discoverer of the path of Dhamma Vinaya, inventor of the satipaṭṭhāna vipassanā meditation technique. If we walk the path discovered and laid down by the Buddha, surely we will reach the intended destination. One who follows Dhamma Vinaya will eventually become flawless.

Our benefactor has shown the path; now, if we walk the path ourselves, we will become the second type of rare and precious being, the being who shows gratitude for what has been given. What the Buddha has given to us is unfathomably precious. If we want to show our gratitude we will practice Dhamma Vinaya systematically.

We need not travel alone down a road of uncertain destination. The Buddha is our guide. He walked this path before us, marked it clearly so that we might follow it well and safely. This is no ordinary road, nor a wrong or misguided one. It is a good path, the correct method, and perfectly safe. Its destination is nibbāna, perfect safety and freedom. Walk the path systematically and you are bound to reach the goal.

A student owes gratitude to his or her teacher; for unselfishly pointing out the path, providing encouragement, and correcting and preventing errors. At the same time he or she owes the Buddha even more. Some students feel gratitude to a living teacher, as a person. However, the teacher, too, must place gratitude where it is due. The teacher who is alive today did not invent this path. He or she merely endeavors to remain faithful to the way as it was laid down and shown by the Buddha. The Buddha instituted the Dhamma Vinaya of the wise. Since his death, it has been very carefully and faithfully handed down from one generation of teachers to the next generation of students. The duty of any teacher is to hand on the Dhamma Vinaya as carefully as he or she has received it. If teachers do not do this work carefully and accurately, the Buddha's original teachings will be lost. There will be no experienced students, and in turn no more qualified teachers who can preserve the tradition and hand it on to further generations.

To know the value of the Dhamma one must practice it first. After it has been well practiced, it can be taught. If it is properly taught, it will continue to flourish. Other methods will not come in. If the practice of Dhamma does not disappear, beings will be happy. This happiness is the value and the meaning of the Dhamma.

Hand in hand, teacher and meditators walk along the path. If we walk this path we will surely reach the place of safety, *khemanta bhūmi.* But we must really cultivate what we have heard, for if the path is known and there are no practitioners, the teaching will fall apart. Other ways will spring up here and there, while the original way will fall into disuse. And if the practice of Dhamma Vinaya declines it will lead to the decline of beings. Beings will end up suffering. As a teacher, one dreads the suffering of one's students. One fears that the moral standards of beings will be destroyed. Therefore, a teacher constantly leads and encourages others on the path. He or she does not want them to encounter disaster and difficulties.

One cannot understand the real value of the practice without taking it on. Unfortunately, there is no pill one can take to alter the mind, no washing machine that can purify meditators. Everyone must invest their own effort and develop their own concentration, then they will understand freedom. It must be done by each of us, but we can all walk this beautiful path together. If we do so, we are bound to reach the destination.

Satipaṭṭhāna vipassanā is a most wonderful path. As it is said in the texts, "This is the direct way for the purification of beings, for the ending of sorrow and lamentation, for the destruction of physical suffering and mental distress, for entry into the right path, and for the attainment of nibbāna." If we guard mindfulness at every moment and practice with diligence, we will come to know the truth of these statements.

Dhamma uplifts us from a low place, and Dhamma saves us. Vinaya dispels any form of polluted behavior. If we continue to practice Dhamma Vinaya, we will reach a place free from defilements. We will know liberation in accordance with the extent of our practice.

A person who walks this path in a straightforward manner will gain all of the qualities of the Noble Eightfold Path, which leads to destruction of the āsavas, or taints. There will be pure and noble morality, pure and noble concentration, pure and noble wisdom. If one does not indulge defilements, one will experience freedom. The Buddha has taught the Dhamma and discipline. If we do not fall away, the answer is simple. One has to examine oneself and assess to what extent we are established in Dhamma Vinaya. A person who falls away from it will be unfulfilled in liberation.

If we do not practice satipaṭṭhāna vipassanā, we will slip, fall from Dhamma, and go wrong—meaning that we will suffer. If we do not live with discipline we will fall away from Vinaya. We will not experience liberation.

Lacking the four qualities of morality, concentration, wisdom, and liberation—*sīla, samādhi, paññā, vimutti*—actually means falling into suffering. If you are not fulfilled in morality, the transgressive defilements will have a field day. You will torment and mistreat other beings without stop or cure. If you set your mind free to think whatever it wants, you will be obsessed and tormented. If you do not support the growth of wisdom, you will not experience the natural ease of being free from the kilesas. Without the three trainings you won't be freed, and there is no greater loss than the loss of freedom.

Some fall away and remain by themselves; others end up in another belief system, getting picked up by others. *Lokiya mahājana,* ordinary worldly people, are those who don't control body and mind. Such people are also called "thick worldlings." These are the people who have no morality or mental control, and therefore nothing to rely upon. They indulge in all kinds of misconduct, without restraint. Beings qualify as ordinary because they lack restraint; they fall and tumble, suffer, and end up with wounds and bruises. It is important to try not to be included in this category!

However, all beings, apart from arahants, fall away from Dhamma Vinaya from time to time. When the kilesas arise, and one is not free of obsession, one falls away. Generally, anytime people are not mindful, they fall away. Only arahants are fully endowed with morality, concentration, wisdom, and liberation, so that they no longer need to make deliberate efforts. An arahant, male or female, does not fall from Dhamma and Vinaya. A person who has attained a minimum of one Noble Path factor, stream entry, still falls but he or she will not end up with physical bruises and wounds.

One should ensure for oneself that one does not end up on the path of the lokiya mahājanas. Please try to reach at least one path and fruition insight! Make an effort as an individual, or join a group to establish the teaching in yourself—then, please pass it on from one generation to the next. If this happens, the result is only happiness. That is certain.

# 6 *Questions and Answers*

GOOD REASONS to ask questions are if you don't understand something, if the instructions are unclear, or if you need to clarify a point. Bad reasons to ask questions are to oppose the teacher, to give him a hard time, or tease him. Questions should be asked with confidence and courage, in the spirit of a family. Asking questions will deepen the family spirit and the Dhamma spirit.

.....

*I thought of asking a question—and fear of humiliation arose.*

When such mental states arise, they should be noted. All mental states should be noted, whether good or bad. When an object is distinct, it has to be noted. Happiness, sadness, gladness, fear. This answer is very easy.

The questioner's family spirit is weak; therefore, fear easily arises. In a family the children trust the mother and they know she will support them. If the mother has something to say, then the children listen.

When relating to one another and there is fear and unease, and we analyze this, we find there is no confidence, therefore no trust. Friendship cannot grow in such an atmosphere. The children know the mother will always support them, and the mother knows the children won't give her trouble. Whatever needs to be said is said. As a meditator, if we understand that the teacher is not there to give us trouble, then we will bravely ask any questions we need to ask.

When birds find out that human beings aren't going to give them trouble, then they gradually learn to go close to those human beings.

• • • • •

*Can effort be too strong?*

Yes indeed, effort can be in excess when one is too zealous. If you hope for and search for objects, you may lose the actual object of observation. This also will lead to too much thinking. Aiming, vitakka, should be made precise. This will open up the mind.

When objects arise very rapidly, in a series, a meditator can feel barraged. He or she asks himself, "Where are the gaps between all these things—how did I miss the arising of the objects?" He or she often decides to apply more effort. But if there's too much energy and effort it only leads to agitation. Instead of connecting with objects, the mind tends to become wide. It can't stay on the object, and gets agitated instead.

It won't stick, but flies up and all around. Concentration is destroyed; the meditator can't see distinct objects. Tranquility also vanishes when one can't label, observe, and know the nature of the objects.

When observing and knowing are absent, a meditator understands that the practice is not working and that he or she needs to back off. When there are too many objects, restrict the attention a bit and focus closely on rising and falling. After the falling movement, one can place the attention momentarily on the whole sitting posture, and then on the pressure points where the buttocks touch chair or cushion. The notes in this case would be: "Rising, falling, sitting, touching." Or else one can note just "Rising, falling, touching." This can help.

Khaṇika samādhi, moment to moment concentration, comes from sustained mindfulness.

• • • • •

*Why is the rising and falling chosen as the primary object?*

To meditate, concentration is needed. Stillness of mind arises with stillness of the body. One must sit still and observe objects. Beginners observe distinct objects at first; later on they can observe any object.

According to Venerable Mahāsi Sayādaw, more than one primary object is suitable. *Ānāpāna,* the breathing sensations at the nose; the rising and falling of the abdomen; and "sitting, touching" as described in the previous question, all are good. Venerable Mingun Sayādaw, Mahāsi Sayādaw's teacher, used sitting and touching.

According to a Pāḷi expression one should give preference to "distinct" objects. This means that material objects should be observed more than mental objects, since mental objects tend to be less clear. Among the four great elements arising in the body, the element of air, *vāyo-dhātu,* is the most distinct experience. The air element consists of sensations of movement, stiffness, hardness, piercing, and the like. Vāyo-dhātu is predominant in the rising and falling. So we tend to use that as a primary object.

Schoolchildren's lessons should be short and easy.

• • • • •

*Should mettā be used to settle the mind at the beginning of a vipassanā sitting?*

No. In a vipassanā retreat, one should not radiate loving-kindness at the beginning of a sitting. One should label and observe the restlessness of the mind.

During a retreat, five minutes a day is enough for all four guardian meditations, as we have discussed.

• • • • •

*How are the dormant kilesas uprooted, and how does the process unfold?*

The latent or dormant kilesas, or anusaya kilesas, have not yet been uprooted. We use the illustration of a match head. When the right conditions are present the anusaya will turn into obsessive or transgressive kilesas, just as an apparently stable match head erupts into flame when struck.

The anusaya kilesas are uprooted through wisdom, paññā. With insight knowledge the kilesas are put aside. With sotāpatti magga and phala, you get rid of wrong view and are freed from clinging to various views. This is rather profound. These kilesas disappear once and for all. It is not like malaria where you get a high fever every other day.

• • • • •

*What are the best practices and attitudes to extinguish craving?*

Satipaṭṭhāna vipassanā meditation!

• • • • •

*What about walking? Should I give it up if I can do long sitting sessions?*

The balance of energy and concentration is important. If that balance is disturbed, either restlessness or sloth will result. You must make an effort in the observation during sitting and the same during walking. Yet in walking there is a double effort—to keep the mind on the object, and then also the physical effort of walking itself.

When there are many objects arising, it can be good to do longer walking periods, of thirty minutes to one hour. Sittings should generally be one hour, minimum.

The five benefits of walking are as follows:

1. You can go on a journey.
2. You will have lots of energy available.
3. You will have good health. Circulation slows if you only sit.
4. You will have good digestion.
5. Durable concentration will develop. Carried into the sitting, it will be easy to develop insight knowledge.

• • • • •

*Are the insight knowledges all the same?*

After stream entry, being freed from wrong views and skeptical doubt, the first through third insight knowledges no longer arise.

These are the insights distinguishing mind and matter, cause and effect, and a preliminary insight into impermanence. If one resumes satipaṭṭhāna vipassanā meditation practice at this point, the progress of insight resumes at the stage of udayabbaya-ñāṇa, insight into the rapid arising and passing away of objects.

A sotāpanna owns *anicca* and *anattā,* impermanence and nonself, and is free of wrongful views. However, she or he has not yet mastered suffering. These people will still come across *saṅkhāra-dukkha,* the suffering inherent in formations, in an outstanding manner.

• • • • •

*How do our lives change with stream entry?*

This is a great question! It is a question that should be answered by a buddha. Monks are not permitted to speak of it, and laypeople should also avoid discussing their profound meditation attainments: it could damage the teaching.

Each one must examine oneself in what we call dhamma-ādāsa, the mirror of the Dhamma. In this mirror one looks at oneself and decides what has taken place. This is the only way.

Still, there is a big difference before and after starting practice. Some students tell me it feels like going from an old to a new life. A woman wrote that she had been looking for the right place all her life and now has found her true home.

Satipaṭṭhāna vipassanā is a sure and certain way to happiness, said the Buddha. We don't need more than his assurance.

• • • • •

*Is it believed that eventually all beings will be enlightened?*

Let us assume you are speaking of "persons," and let us also narrow down the question to whether there will be a time when there are no ordinary worldlings left.

Frankly, this does not seem likely to happen anytime soon.

Those who are close to the Buddha and Dhamma, and who have perfected the pāramīs, will gain the special Dhamma. Developing pāramīs is done in every existence. Yogis and meditators are practicing to gain the Dhamma—if they don't succeed, then the work remains to be done in another existence. If they laid the groundwork in a previous existence, they can complete their task in this one.

Developing pāramīs means performing acts of wholesomeness: generosity, morality, renunciation, wisdom, energy, patience, truthfulness, resolution, loving-kindness, and equanimity. Do so without self-interest; work for the benefit of others. If the goal or objective is to benefit others, or for the attainment of nibbāna, then such deeds are truly wholesome. Development of the perfections is very important.

Another very important practice for liberation is *atta-sammāpaṇiddhi,* proper self-regulation. You must shape your physical, verbal, and mental behavior to be free from flaws, to be lovely and well formed—but you must do so with a particular view toward developing the mind for knowledge. To be able to regulate oneself successfully one must rely on a kalyāṇa mitta, a spiritual friend, in other words, a qualified teacher. One must also be in a place where Dhamma Vinaya is well propagated.

These indispensable conditions—living in a place where the teachings are available, meeting the wise, and having the opportunity to shape oneself—all come from past good actions.

• • • • •

*What is the most important theoretical and practical thing to know in order to realize nibbāna?*

To realize nibbāna, path and fruition consciousness are needed. Ordinary worldly consciousness cannot realize nibbāna. So *magga* and *phala,* path and fruition, are needed. Magga is the destruction, cutting off, or extinguishing of defilements. Phala is a repeated extinguishing of the fire, like a cooling of the ashes. If a fire is very big, one first extinguishes it and then soaks it with much more water in the second round.

Both magga and phala take nibbāna as an object. Magga takes nibbāna as an object, while phala takes the extinguished fire as an object and extinguishes it totally.

The first path and fruition consciousnesses are called sotāpatti magga and sotāpatti phala, the path and fruition of stream entry. After stream entry there are three more levels of liberation.

Sotāpatti extinguishes three fetters—*sakkāya diṭṭhi,* the belief in an enduring self essence, together with *vicikicchā,* skeptical doubt; the idea that one can gain Dhamma through rites and rituals; and the defilements that lead to rebirth in apāya, or states of loss such as hell or the realms of hungry ghosts and animals. Greed, hatred, and delusion are weakened, and it is said that one will have only seven more rebirths. However, other kilesas will linger on, to be dealt with in the higher path and fruition consciousnesses.

All unwholesome actions based on the eradicated kilesas will stop. When there are no more kilesas, the actions will stop; the results then stop as well.

In order to gain final peace, one will have to develop small fractions of peace in the early stages of practice. We must guard the mind in every moment of arising. Satipaṭṭhāna vipassanā means an intense observation of distinct targets, namely, the four foundations or "establishments" of mindfulness. We observe physical sensations; we observe pleasant, unpleasant, and neutral feelings; we observe mental activities like thinking and planning; and we observe all general activities.

In an intensive retreat or a formal sitting practice, awareness is anchored in the rising and falling movement of the abdomen. In the rising, there will be tension and the knowing of tension. If the rising is seen in this manner, this is right view. Anytime the mind is properly aligned with the target of observation it will be free from wrongful thoughts and intentions, *micchā sankappa.*

Sati, or mindfulness, needs help from other mental factors as we have seen. Most important is viriya, which has the nature of distancing the defilements. Once this has been done, sati protects the mind, and samādhi unites it. With these three factors, viriya, sati, and samādhi, there can be momentary peace.

Sīla, or morality, extinguishes the transgressive defilements. Samādhi, or concentration, suppresses the obsessive defilements. Paññā, or wisdom, cuts off the latent or anusaya defilements. As one practices, one progresses through the insight knowledges and ends up in magga-phala. With sincere practice, the pubbe-bhāga-magga, the forerunner path, can be fulfilled. This forerunner path consists of nothing other than satipaṭṭhāna vipassanā, direct observation of objects as and when they arise.

One must also associate with the wise, be straightforward in practice, and practice to completion. These three factors are very important.

• • • • •

*If consciousness dies at death, then how does kamma continue from birth to birth?*

One moment of consciousness arises and it disappears right away. So death is nothing unusual. The last moment of consciousness in a life is the death consciousness, *cuti citta.* It leaves nothing behind and is immediately followed by *paṭisandhi citta,* the first consciousness of the next existence.

Some think the consciousness is jumping from one existence to the next. It is not like this. You may be familiar with a seal that leaves a mark or impression on paper. The connection between the seal and its mark is like the connection between cuti citta and paṭisandhi citta. It is also like an echo of a loud sound in a cave. The echo is not the original sound, but it is related to the sound.

Similar is the link between an old and a new existence. In any case, the three vaṭṭas continue to turn, until avijjā is destroyed.

• • • • •

*Is it correct to say that the latent kilesas are all the object-related kilesas not cut off by path and fruition consciousness?*

The *ārammāṇa-anusaya kilesas,* or object-related kilesas, are the defilements of all the objects at the six sense doors. These have not been dispelled at the sotāpanna stage. They, and other latent kilesas known as the defilements of the life continuum, support each other.

However, they are temporarily extinguished during the forerunner path, that is, during vipassanā meditation practice.

. . . . .

*What should we do when we leave a retreat?*
*How important is it to read books and listen to Dhamma talks between retreats? Should we support monks and Dhamma teachers? And what about morality?*

When you leave a retreat, the most important thing to do is to carry this practice along to your home. If you take the Dhamma home but don't practice, you will lose and destroy the habits you so carefully built up during the retreat. In daily life, you must learn to set aside the time for formal meditation sessions, while of course also leaving time for other activities. One hour a day is a minimum to develop one's skills further. If you want to attend further retreats in the future, it is also good to maintain an hour per day, or even more, if you can. Then, when you arrive at a retreat you will maximize the benefit you can reap in the limited time you have available.

Meditation is similar to playing the piano. Even highly accomplished players always maintain hours of practice. Great athletes, too, spend a lot of time on the training field.

Think of yourself as a patient suffering from a disease, who has had to be hospitalized. When you leave the hospital, the doctors will recommend a special diet and medicine. If you, the patient, adhere to these recommendations, then your disease will be cured. So don't leave the medicine behind when you go home!

As for reading books, ordinary books will not at all contribute to Dhamma progress. Even among Dhamma books it is no good to read in an unselected manner, here and there. One should seek out books that give precise meditation instructions. By reading books that present the correct scriptures you will come to know what you did not, and deepen knowledge that you already had. Reading Dhamma books also dispels doubts and straightens out certain problems. It has many benefits, though in itself reading books is not a cause for the arising and increasing of insight. Only direct observation will do that.

Approaching and supporting Buddhist teachers and monastics is also appropriate and necessary. These teachers should be genuine, though—only then is it good to support them.

As for practicing sīla, if morality is broken, one cannot establish correct mindfulness. Only if morality is kept will meditation become possible. The field of Dhamma discipline has three sikkhās, which we have discussed extensively. Every one of them gives benefits. Morality is the foundation of Dhamma practice. One cannot skip past sīla. Nor can one go directly to *paññā,* wisdom, without developing concentration. You need all three.

• • • • •

*Can you give us more guidance for refining our noting practice? Can you give an example of a powerful single note?*

You have to get *very* close to the object to see it well.

In the body, distinct objects arise. They all have to be known distinctly and clearly. They arise and pass, arise and pass. Heat is not just one thing but a series of heat sensations. First it is seen as a composite, then you recognize that it is breaking up.

Send the mind toward the object. Align with it. As sati gets closer and closer it gets better and better. The object will be seen in great detail.

A line of ants, from far away, is seen as a dark line across the road. As one gradually approaches, one sees it wavering slightly and then that it is composed of many, many individual ants. Crouching down, one begins to make out individual ants, with spaces between them—in fact it is no longer so much a line that one is perceiving, for that concept has dropped away. At some point one can appreciate the antennae, the six legs, and three sections of a single ant's body, and maybe some small crumb it is carrying in its jaws.

• • • • •

*When is it better to cut off thoughts or sensations and when should one continue to note them?*

It is never taught that you should cut off an object. When wandering mind arises, it should be noted, not cut off. Only the defilements are to be cut off. First they must be observed, and then cut. This generally means not remaining involved with them.

The instruction says, "*Bhūta bhūtāti passato,* see existing things as they are." The instruction does not say, cut things off!

However, if wandering mind arises too often or strongly, and you become weary, you may set it aside and contemplate another object. Physical objects should be noted. But one can get wearied of one particular object after some time. If this happens, just put it aside.

In general, noting objects as and when they occur in the present moment is always best.

• • • • •

*How do we know when noting is good?*

When noting is good, objects seem to arise automatically. You don't feel you have to go looking for them. It is like playing the piano—you reach a stage where you no longer need advice.

• • • • •

*Where does this fall in the stages of insight—when the suffering is so intense, the mind lets go of the object and then there is release from suffering, and then it is seen only as a mental and physical process, empty in essence?*

Some meditators study the stages. Some meditators want to know the answer in advance. In a mathematical formula, is it the formula that is important, or the answer?

Listen to the formula, and learn how to make the calculation. Then, do the calculation yourself. An answer given, without having made the calculation yourself, will not be accepted by the teacher.

The formula has been given. If you make a personal calculation, this is good. Otherwise you may go wrong and it becomes a Dhamma danger.

• • • • •

*Is something lacking in a practitioner's development if he or she has no questions?*

Please don't think that progress depends on whether you have questions or don't have questions. Knowing the object from moment to moment is what constitutes progress. You are not lacking in anything.

Taste for yourself tranquility and the other results of meditation practice. Don't ask questions just to ask—it will interfere. But if you don't understand something, then by all means ask!

The mind becomes clear and calm. If you practice steadily the Noble Eightfold Path will develop. Then you will no longer need to ask questions.

Your question is not a sign of a flaw. If someone offers you food and you ask about its origins, you won't taste the food. So, continue to eat!

• • • • •

In conclusion, I would like to remind you that all of you are in a frontline battle against the defilements. If you don't fight, you will be overrun by the kilesa enemy. Your commander says, "Go out and fight!"

# *English–Pāḷi Glossary*

| | |
|---|---|
| absorption, meditative | jhāna |
| action, intentional | kamma |
| cycle of action | kamma vaṭṭa |
| adherence due to thick delusion; bewilderment | sammoha-abhinivesa |
| affection toward near and dear ones | pema |
| aiming, concentration factor of | vitakka |
| anger | dosa |
| anger; hatred; malice | āghāta |
| association with a knowledgeable person | sappurisa-saṃseva |
| attachment, subtle (often to meditation experience) | nikanti |
| attainment of the cause of buddhahood | hetu-sampadā |
| attention | mānasikāra |
| unwise, ill-directed | ayoniso-mānasikāra |
| wise | yoniso-mānasikāra |
| being | satta |
| breathing (living) | pāṇa |
| celestial | deva |
| living; distinctly existing | bhūta |
| belief in an enduring self essence | sakkāya diṭṭhi |
| benefactor | upakārī |
| body | kāya |
| breath; breathing sensations | ānāpāna |

| | |
|---|---|
| buddha, silent; one who is enlightened but does not teach the truth to the world | paccekabuddha |
| cause, proximate | padaṭṭhāna |
| celestial being; deity | deva |
| characteristic | lakkhaṇa |
| of non-superficiality | apilāpana lakkhaṇa |
| clairvoyance | dibba-cakkhu-ñāṇa |
| clear comprehension | sampajañña |
| clinging | upādāna |
| compassion | karuṇā |
| great | mahā karuṇā |
| conceit and pride | māna |
| concentration | samādhi |
| group (of the Noble Eightfold Path) | samādhi khandha |
| momentary | khaṇika samādhi |
| nondistracted | avikkhepa samādhi |
| Right | sammā-samādhi |
| teaching of | samādhi sāsana |
| training in | samādhi sikkhā |
| concept | paññatti |
| concept of manner | ākāra-paññatti |
| conduct, basic | caraṇa |
| confidence | saddhā |
| consciousness | citta |
| of death | cuti citta |
| rebirth-linking | paṭisandhi citta |
| contact (of mind with an object) | phassa |

| | |
|---|---|
| contemplation | anupassanā |
| of feelings as an establishment of mindfulness | vedanānupassanā satipaṭṭhāna |
| of impurity or foulness | asubha bhāvanā |
| of virtues of the Dhamma | dhammānussati |
| continuously rushing (toward an object) | pakkhanditvā pavattati |
| craving | taṇhā |
| cultivation; mental development | bhāvanā |
| cycle | vaṭṭa |
| of existence | saṃsāra |
| of (kammic) results | vipāka vaṭṭa |
| death, mindfulness of | maraṇasati |
| defilement or distortion of mind | kilesa |
| cycle of | kilesa vaṭṭa |
| dormant or latent | anusaya kilesa |
| as enemy | kilesa vera |
| flowing into the mind | āsava kilesa |
| object-related | ārammāṇa-anusaya kilesa |
| obsessive | pariyuṭṭhāna kilesa |
| realm of | kilesa bhūmi |
| transgressive | vītikkama kilesa |
| delusion | moha, sammoha |
| desire | lobha |
| desire, sensual | kāma-cchanda |
| desire (to act or practice, excluding greed or lust) | chanda |
| desire to torment others | vihiṁsa-vitakka |
| desirous to acquire knowledge | ñātukāma |
| Dhamma speech | Sutta |
| Dhamma success or Dhamma victory | dhamma-vijaya |
| disciple | sāvaka |

| | |
|---|---|
| disciple in training | sekha |
| discipline | vinaya |
| discourse (of the Buddha) | Sutta |
| discriminating knowledge | paṭisambhidā |
| disease of the mind | mānasikaroga |
| distinctly existing mind-body process | sa-kāya or sakkāya |
| divine eye | dibba cakkhu |
| doubt, skeptical | vicikicchā |
| downfall; falling away | papatita |
| effort | viriya |
| ardent | ātāpa |
| continuously uplifting | paggahita viriya |
| fulfilled | paripuṇṇa viriya |
| element of air | vāyo-dhātu |
| enemy; enmity | vera |
| enemy in human form | puggalā vera |
| unwholesomeness as | akusala vera |
| enlightenment knowledge | bodhi-ñāṇa |
| equanimity | upekkhā |
| establishment | upaṭṭhāna |
| of mindfulness (on a type of object) | satipaṭṭhāna |
| of mindfulness, meditation on | satipaṭṭhāna vipassanā |
| extraordinary | visiṭṭha |
| faith | saddhā |
| fear | bhaya |
| of censure by others | parānuvāda-bhaya |
| of consequences, moral; of wrongdoing | ottappa |
| of punishment by authorities | daṇḍa-bhaya |
| of rebirth in an unfavorable existence | duggati-bhaya |
| of self-blame | attānuvāda-bhaya |

| | |
|---|---|
| fearlessness, moral; lack of fear of wrongdoing | anottappa |
| feeling | vedanā |
| contemplation of as an establishment of mindfulness | vedanānupassanā satipaṭṭhāna |
| female being | itthi |
| field | bhūmi |
| flavor of true nature | sabhāva-rasa |
| forerunner or preliminary path | pubbe-bhāga-magga |
| four | catu |
| free from mental suffering | avyāpajjha |
| free from physical suffering | anigha |
| freedom from disturbances based in greed and hatred | gutti |
| freedom from enmity | avera |
| friend, spiritual | kalyāṇa mitta |
| friendly actions performed with the body | kāya-kamma mettā |
| friendly mental actions | mano-kamma mettā |
| fruition | phala |
| accomplishment (attainment) of fruit or result | phala-sampadā |
| fulfillment or perfection of the Buddha's teaching | sāsana sampatti |
| function | rasa |
| future buddha; buddha-to-be | bodhisattā |
| gratitude | kataññutā |
| great passing away (of a buddha) | mahāparinibbāna |
| grief | soka |

| | |
|---|---|
| group | khandha |
| concentration (of the Eightfold Path) | samādhi khandha |
| morality (of the Eightfold Path) | sāla khandha |
| wisdom (of the Eightfold Path) | paññā khandha |
| happiness | sukha |
| of insight | vipassanā-sukha |
| of tranquility | samatha-sukha |
| hatred | dosa |
| haughtiness | atimāna |
| hearing the true Dhamma | saddhamma savaṇa |
| heat element | tejo-dhātu |
| ignorance | avijjā |
| ill-intentioned speech | vacī-duccarita |
| impermanence | anicca |
| inability to see presently arising objects as they truly exist | avibhūta |
| individual being | puggala |
| inoperative | kriyā or kiriya |
| insight, happiness of | vipassanā-sukha |
| insight knowledge (*see also* knowledge) | ñāṇa |
| into rising and passing | udayabbaya-ñāṇa |
| intention | cetanā |
| interest, joyful | pīti |
| kind intention | cetanā-mettā |
| intention to remember what one has heard | dhāretukāma |

| | |
|---|---|
| knowledge | ñāṇa |
| into arising and passing | udayabbaya-ñāṇa |
| of discernment | paṭisambhidā-ñāṇa |
| omniscient | sabbaññutā-ñāṇa |
| and seeing | ñāṇa-dassana |
| of teaching | desanā-ñāṇa |
| knowledge and conduct | vijjā-caraṇa |
| liberation | vimutti |
| listener | sāvaka |
| love of home or family | gehasita-pema |
| loving-kindness | mettā |
| meditation on | mettā bhāvanā |
| nonspecific pervasion of | anodiso pharaṇa mettā |
| perfected | mettā-pāramīs |
| specific pervasion of | odiso pharaṇa mettā |
| lust | rāga |
| madness based on hatred; blind rage | kodhummattaka |
| male being | purisa |
| manifestation | paccupaṭṭhāna |
| matter | rūpa |
| meditation, insight | vipassanā bhāvanā |
| on the establishments of mindfulness | satipaṭṭhāna vipassanā bhāvanā |
| meditation, protective or guardian | ārakkhā bhāvanā |
| meditation or mental development | bhāvanā |
| meditative absorption | jhāna |
| mental actions complemented and strengthened by verbal and bodily actions | hitūpasaṁhāra-rasa |
| mental defilement as enemy | kilesa vera |
| mental factor | cetasika |
| mettā, verbal acts of | vacī-kamma mettā |

| | |
|---|---|
| mind | nāma |
| mind and body | nāma-rūpa |
| mind object; thing | dhamma |
| mind state; state of consciousness | citta |
| mindfulness | sati |
| intensive | bhusattha sati |
| of death | maraṇasati |
| right | sammā-sati |
| mindfulness, establishment of | satipaṭṭhāna |
| contemplation of body | kāyānupassanā satipaṭṭhāna |
| contemplation of dhamma | dhammānupassanā satipaṭṭhāna |
| contemplation of feeling | vedanānupassanā satipaṭṭhāna |
| contemplation of states of mind | cittānupassanā satipaṭṭhāna |
| mirror of the dhamma | dhamma-ādāsa |
| misconduct | duccarita |
| performed through speech | vacī-duccarita |
| performed through the body | kāya duccarita |
| performed through the mind | mano duccarita |
| morality | sīla |
| group (of the Noble Eightfold Path) | sīla khandha |
| teaching of | sīla sāsana |
| training in | sīla sikkhā |
| negligence; carelessness; heedlessness | pamāda |
| neutrality of mind | tatra-majjhattatā |
| noble one | ariyā |
| noble practice | brahmacariyā |
| non-forgetfulness, function of | asammosa rasa |
| non-human being | amanussa |
| non-noble being | anariya |
| nondistracted concentration | avikkhepa samādhi |
| nonhatred | adosa |

| | |
|---|---|
| nonreturner | anāgāmī |
| nonself | anattā |
| once-returner; the second stage of liberation | sakadāgāmī |
| outstanding | visiṭṭha |
| owner of one's actions | kammassaka |
| path | magga |
| and fruition of holiness | arahatta magga phala |
| leading to the exhaustion of defilements | sammādukkhakkhayagāmā |
| of stream entry | sotāpatti magga |
| peace | santi |
| perception | saññā |
| perfection | pāramīs |
| of loving-kindness | mettā-pāramīs |
| person | puggala |
| person who is dear | piyamanāpa-puggala |
| perversion of perception | saññā-vipallāsa |
| continuously moving forward | okkantitvā pavattati |
| power | bala |
| practice that is in accordance with Dhamma Vinaya | dhammānudhamma paṭipatti |
| pride and conceit | māna |
| protection of the mind from defilements | ārakkhā paccupaṭṭhāna |
| pure vision | āsavakkhaya-ñāṇa |
| purification of view | diṭṭhi-visuddhi |
| purity; mental purification | visuddhi |
| quivering of the mind | anukampā |
| rage | kodhummattaka |
| realm | bhūmi |
| rebirth-linking consciousness | paṭisandhi citta |

| | |
|---|---|
| rebirth into a new existence | paṭisandhi |
| recollection | anussati |
| of past existences | pubbe-nivāsa-anussati |
| of virtues of the Buddha | buddhānussati |
| requisites of enlightenment | bodhipakkhiyā dhammā |
| restlessness and worry | uddhacca-kukkucca |
| results, cycle of vipāka | vaṭṭa |
| right Action | sammā-kammanta |
| right Aim | sammā-sankappa |
| right Concentration | sammā-samādhi |
| right Effort | sammā-vāyāma |
| right Livelihood | sammā-ājīva |
| right Mindfulness | sammā-sati |
| right Speech | sammā-vācā |
| right View | sammā-diṭṭhi |
| rubbing or sustaining, concentration factor of | vicāra |
| safety, realm or field of | khemanta bhūmi |
| seeing and knowing in accordance with reality | yathā-bhūta-ñāṇa-dassana |
| self | jīva-atta |
| self-regulation | atta-sammāpaṇidhi |
| self-view | atta-diṭṭhi |
| sensual desire | kāma-cchanda |
| sensuous thought | kāma-vitakka |
| shame, moral | hiri |
| shamelessness; lack of moral shame | ahirika |
| skeptical doubt | vicikicchā |
| skillful speech | vacī-sucarita |
| skimming or wobbling | pilāpana |
| sloth and torpor | thīna-middha |

| | |
|---|---|
| soul | jīva-atta |
| speech | vācana |
| speech, skillful | vacī-sucarita |
| state of loss such as hell | apāya |
| stream; succession; continuity | santāna |
| stream entry | sotāpatti |
| stream entry, path of | sotāpatti magga |
| stream-enterer; the first stage of liberation | sotāpanna |
| strong determination to save oneself and others | mutto-moceyyaṁ |
| strong perception; the recording or recognition of objects as approximate cause | thirasaññā padaṭṭhāna |
| suffering | dukkha |
| inherent in formations | sankhāra-dukkha |
| truth of | dukkha-sacca |
| suffering being | dukkhita |
| suffusion or pervasion | pharaṇa |
| supreme being or spirit | parama-atta |
| sympathetic joy | muditā |
| teaching | sāsana |
| fulfillment or perfection of | sāsana sampatti |
| of concentration | samādhi sāsana |
| of morality | sīla sāsana |
| teaching and discipline (of the Buddha) | Dhamma Vinaya |
| teaching, basic | caraṇa |
| teachings about existence | Dhamma |
| tendencies, habitual (kammic) | vāsanā |
| thing | dhamma |
| thought of hatred and ill will | vyāpāda-vitakka |

| | |
|---|---|
| training | sikkhā |
| in concentration | samādhi sikkhā |
| in morality | sīla sikkhā |
| transgressive defilements | vītikkama kilesa |
| true nature; the way of being | sabhāva |
| flavor of | sabhāva-rasa |
| truth about existence; teaching about existence | Dhamma |
| truthless | adhamma |
| ultimate reality | paramattha-dhamma |
| undertaking | payoga |
| unlimited abode | brahmavihāra |
| unwholesomeness enemy | akusala vera |
| verbal acts of mettā | vacī-kamma mettā |
| view that sees distinct mind and matter | sa-kāya-diṭṭhi |
| vision; knowledge | vijjā |
| wisdom | paññā |
| field of | paññā bhūmi |
| group (of the Noble Eightfold Path) | paññā khandha |
| teaching of | paññā sāsana |
| training in | paññā sikkhā |
| wise attention | yoniso-mānasikāra |
| wish to hear the Dhamma | sotukāma |
| work for others' benefit | parahita |
| work for the benefit of relatives and fellow citizens | ñātatthacariyā |
| work for the benefit of the world | lokatthacariyā |
| work toward becoming a buddha; developing of the pāramīs | buddhatthacariyā |
| worldling; worldly person | puthujjana, lokiya mahājana |
| wrong intention | micchā sankappa |

# *Pāḷi–English Glossary*

| | |
|---|---|
| adhamma | truthless |
| adosa | nonhatred |
| ahirika | moral shamelessness, lack of moral shame |
| āghāta | anger, hatred, malice |
| ākāra-paññatti | concept of manner |
| akusala vera | unwholesomeness enemy |
| amanussa | inhuman beings, persons who lack basic morality |
| anāgāmī | nonreturner, the third stage of liberation |
| ānāpāna | breath, breathing sensations |
| anariya | non-noble being |
| anattā | nonself |
| anicca | impermanence |
| anigha | free from physical suffering |
| anodiso pharaṇa mettā | unlimited radiation of loving-kindness, nonspecific pervasion of loving-kindness |
| anottappa | moral fearlessness, lack of fear of wrongdoing |
| anukampā | quivering of mind |
| anupassanā | contemplation |
| anusaya kilesa | dormant or latent defilement |
| apāya | fearful realms, states of loss such as hell |
| apilāpana lakkhaṇa | characteristic of non-superficiality, cf. pilāpana |
| arahatta magga phala | path and fruition of holiness |
| ārakkhā bhāvanā | protective meditations, guardian meditations |

| | |
|---|---|
| ārakkhā paccupaṭṭhāna | protecting the mind from defilements, manifestation of |
| ārammāṇa-anusaya kilesa | object-related defilement |
| ariyā | a noble one |
| asammosa rasa | non-forgetfulness, keeping the object in view |
| āsava kilesa | defilements that flow into the mind |
| āsavakkhaya-ñāṇa | pure vision |
| asubha bhāvanā | contemplation of impurity or foulness |
| ātāpa | ardent effort |
| atimāna | conceited haughtiness |
| atta-diṭṭhi | self-view |
| atta-sammā-paṇiddhi | proper self-regulation |
| attānuvāda-bhaya | fear or danger of self-blame |
| avera | freedom from enmity |
| avibhūta | inability to see presently arising objects as they truly exist |
| avijjā | ignorance, delusion |
| avikkhepa samādhi | nondistracted concentration |
| avyāpajjha | free from mental suffering |
| ayoniso-mānasikāra | ill-directed attention |
| bala | power |
| bhāvanā | meditation, cultivation |
| bhaya | fear, danger |
| bhusattha sati | intensive mindfulness |
| bhūmi | field, realm |
| bhūta | living being, distinctly existing being |
| bodhi-ñāṇa | enlightenment knowledge |
| bodhipakkhiyā dhammā | requisites of enlightenment |
| bodhisattā | future buddha, buddha-to-be |

| | |
|---|---|
| brahmacariyā | noble practice |
| brahmavihāra | unlimited abode |
| buddhānussati | recollection of the virtues of the Buddha |
| buddhatthacariyā | working toward becoming a buddha, developing of the pāramīs |
| caraṇa | basic teaching or basic conduct |
| catu | four |
| cetanā | intention |
| cetanā-mettā | kind intention |
| cetasika | mental factor |
| chanda | desire to act or practice, excluding greed or lust |
| citta | mind state, state of consciousness |
| cittānupassanā satipaṭṭhāna | contemplation of the states of mind as an establishment of mindfulness |
| cuti citta | death consciousness |
| daṇḍa-bhaya | fear of punishment by authorities |
| desanā-ñāṇa | knowledge of teaching |
| deva | celestial beings |
| dhamma | mind object, thing |
| Dhamma | truth about existence; teaching about existence |
| dhamma-ādāsa | mirror of the dhamma, dhamma mirror |
| Dhamma Vinaya | teaching and discipline (of the Buddha) |
| dhamma-vijaya | Dhamma success or Dhamma victory |
| dhammānudhamma paṭipatti | practice that is in accordance with Dhamma Vinaya |
| dhammānupassanā satipaṭṭhāna | contemplation of mind objects as an establishment of mindfulness |
| dhammānussati | contemplation of the virtues of the Dhamma |
| dhāretukāma | intention to remember what one has heard |
| dibba cakkhu | divine eye |

| | |
|---|---|
| dibba-cakkhu-ñāṇa | clairvoyance |
| diṭṭhi-visuddhi | purification of view |
| dosa | hatred, anger |
| duccarita | misconduct |
| duggati-bhaya | fear of being reborn in an unfavorable existence |
| dukkhita | suffering being |
| dukkha-sacca | Noble Truth of Suffering |
| gehasita-pema | love of home or family |
| gutti | freedom from disturbances based in greed and hatred |
| hetu-sampadā | attainment of the cause of buddhahood |
| hitūpasaṁhāra-rasa | mental actions complemented and strengthened by verbal and bodily actions |
| hiri | moral shame |
| itthi | female being |
| jhāna | meditative absorption |
| jīva-atta | soul or self |
| kalyāṇa mitta | spiritual friend |
| kāma-cchanda | sensual desire |
| kāma-vitakka | sensuous thought |
| kamma | intentional action |
| kamma vaṭṭa | cycle of actions |
| kammassaka | owner of one's actions |
| kammassakāta sammā-diṭṭhi | the right view that beings are owners of karma |
| karuṇā | compassion |
| kataññū | those who return gratitude for what they have |
| kāya | body |
| kāya duccarita | misconduct performed through the body |
| kāya-kamma mettā | friendly actions performed with the body |

| | |
|---|---|
| kāyānupassanā satipaṭṭhāna | contemplation of the body as an establishment of mindfulness |
| khaṇika samādhi | momentary concentration, moment to moment concentration |
| khemanta bhūmi | place of safety |
| kilesa | defilement, distortion of mind |
| kilesa bhūmi | realm of the kilesas |
| kilesa vaṭṭa | cycle of defilement or affliction |
| kilesa vera | mental disturbance enemy |
| kodhummattaka | mental madness based on hatred, blind rage |
| kiriya | inoperative |
| lakkhaṇa | characteristic |
| lobha | craving, desire, lust |
| lokatthacariyā | working for the benefit of the world |
| lokiya mahājana | ordinary worldly person |
| magga | path |
| mahā karuṇā | great compassion |
| mahāparinibbāna | great passing away (of a buddha) |
| māna | pride and conceit |
| manasikāra | attention |
| mānasikaroga | disease of the mind |
| mano duccarita | misconduct performed through the mind |
| mano-kamma mettā | friendly mental actions |
| maraṇasati | mindfulness of death |
| mettā | loving-kindness |
| mettā bhāvanā | loving-kindness meditation |
| mettā-pāramīs | perfected loving-kindness |
| miccha sankappa | wrong intention |
| moha | delusion |

| | |
|---|---|
| muditā | sympathetic joy |
| mutto-moceyyaṁ | strong determination to save oneself and others |
| nāma | mind |
| nāma-rūpa | mind and body |
| ñāṇa | insight knowledge |
| ñāṇa-dassana | knowing and seeing, perfect knowledge |
| ñātatthacariyā | working for the benefit of relatives and fellow citizens |
| ñātukāma | desire to acquire knowledge, anxious to know |
| nikanti | subtle attachment |
| odiso pharaṇa mettā | unlimited radiation of loving-kindness |
| okkantitvā pavattati | continuously moving forward |
| ottappa | moral fear, fear of consequences |
| paccekabuddha | one who is enlightened but does not teach the truth to the world |
| paccupaṭṭhāna | manifestation |
| padaṭṭhāna | proximate cause |
| paggahita viriya | continuously uplifting effort |
| pakkhanditvā pavattati | rushing or springing forward (toward a mental object) |
| pamāda | negligence, carelessness, heedlessness |
| pāṇa | breathing being, living being |
| paññā | wisdom |
| paññā bhūmi | field of wisdom |
| paññā khandha | wisdom group (of the Noble Eightfold Path) |
| paññā sāsana | teaching of wisdom |
| paññā sikkhā | training in wisdom |
| paññatti | concept |
| papatita | downfall, falling away |
| parahita | work for others' benefit |

| | |
|---|---|
| parama-atta | supreme being or spirit |
| paramattha-dhamma | ultimate reality |
| pāramīs | perfection |
| parānuvāda-bhaya | fear of censure by others |
| paripuṇṇa-viriya | fulfilled effort |
| pariyuṭṭhāna kilesa | obsessive mental defilements |
| paṭisambhidā ñāṇa | knowledge of discernment, discriminating knowledge |
| paṭisandhi | rebirth into a new existence |
| paṭisandhi citta | rebirth-linking consciousness |
| payoga | practice, undertaking, action |
| pema | attachment to near and dear ones |
| phala | fruition |
| phala-sampadā | accomplishment of result |
| pharaṇa | suffusion or pervasion |
| phassa | contact (of mind with an object) |
| pilāpana | skimming or wobbling |
| pīti | joyful interest |
| piyamanāpa-puggala | dear person |
| pubbe-bhāga-magga | forerunner or preliminary path |
| pubbe-nivāsa-anussati | recollection of past existences |
| puggala | individual being, person |
| puggalā vera | enemies in human form |
| purisa | male being |
| puthujjana | worldling |
| rāga | lust |
| rasa | function |
| rūpa | matter |
| sa-kāya, sakkāya | distinctly existing mind-body process |

| | |
|---|---|
| sa-kāya-diṭṭhi | view that sees distinct mind and matter |
| sabbe | all |
| sabbe sattā | all beings |
| sabbaññutā-ñāṇa | omniscient knowledge |
| sabhāva | true nature, the way of being |
| sabhāva-rasa | flavor of true nature |
| saddhā | faith, confidence |
| saddhamma savaṇa | hearing the true dhamma |
| sakadāgāmī | once-returner, the second stage of liberation |
| sakkāya diṭṭhi | belief in an enduring self essence |
| samādhi | concentration |
| samādhi khandha | concentration group (of the Noble Eightfold Path) |
| samādhi sāsana | teaching of concentration |
| samādhi sikkhā | training in concentration |
| samatha-sukha | happiness of tranquility |
| sammā-ājīva | right Livelihood |
| sammā-diṭṭhi | right View |
| sammā-kammanta | right Action |
| sammā-samādhi | right Concentration |
| sammā-sankappa | right Aim |
| sammā-sati | right Mindfulness |
| sammā-vācā | right Speech |
| sammā-vāyāma | right Effort |
| sammādukkhakkhayagāmī | leading to the exhaustion of defilements |
| sammoha | delusion |
| sammoha-abhinivesa | adherence due to thick delusion, bewilderment |
| sampajañña ñāṇa dassana | clear, directly evident, and distinct comprehension; knowing and seeing; perfect knowledge |

| | |
|---|---|
| saṃsāra | cycle of existence |
| santāna | stream, succession, continuity |
| sankhāra-dukkha | suffering inherent in formations |
| saññā | perception |
| sañña-vipallāsa | perversion of perception |
| santi | peace |
| sappurisa-saṃseva | association with a knowledgeable person |
| sāsana | teaching |
| sāsana sampatti | fulfillment or perfection of the Buddha's teaching |
| sati | mindfulness |
| satipaṭṭhāna | foundation of mindfulness |
| satipaṭṭhāna vipassanā bhāvanā | mental development through mindfulness meditation |
| satta | being |
| sāvaka | disciple, listener |
| sekha | disciple, someone in training |
| sikkhā | training |
| sīla | morality |
| sīla khandha | morality group (of the Noble Eightfold Path) |
| sīla sāsana | teaching of morality |
| sīla sikkhā | training in morality |
| soka | grief |
| sotāpanna | stream-enterer, the first stage of liberation |
| sotāpatti | stream entry |
| sotāpatti magga | path of stream entry |
| ṣotukāma | wish to hear the Dhamma |
| Sutta | discourse |
| taṇhā | craving |
| tatra-majjhattatā | neutrality of mind |

| | |
|---|---|
| tejo-dhātu | heat element |
| thīna-middha | sloth and torpor |
| thirasaññā padaṭṭhāna | strong perception, the recording or recognition of objects |
| udayabbaya-ñāṇa | insight into rising and passing |
| uddhacca-kukkucca | restlessness and worry |
| upādāna | clinging |
| upakārī | benefactor |
| upaṭṭhāna | establishment |
| upekkhā | equanimity |
| vācana | speech |
| vacī-duccarita | ill-intentioned speech |
| vacī-sucarita | skillful speech |
| vacī-kamma mettā | verbal acts of mettā |
| vāsanā | kammic tendencies |
| vaṭṭa | cycle |
| vāyo-dhātu | element of air |
| vedanā | feeling |
| vedanānupassanā satipaṭṭhāna | contemplation of feelings as an establishment of mindfulness |
| vera | enemy |
| vicāra | rubbing, concentration factor of sustaining |
| vicikicchā | skeptical doubt |
| vihiṁsa-vitakka | desire to torment others |
| vijjā | vision, knowledge |
| vijjā-caraṇa | knowledge and conduct |
| vimutti | liberation |
| vinaya | discipline or training |
| vipāka vaṭṭa | cycle of results |

| | |
|---|---|
| vipassanā-sukha | happiness of insight |
| viriya | effort |
| visiṭṭha | outstanding, extraordinary |
| visuddhi | purity, (mental) purification |
| vitakka | concentration factor of aiming |
| vītikkama kilesa | transgressive defilements |
| vyāpāda-vitakka | thought of hatred and ill will |
| yathā-bhūta-ñāṇa-dassana | seeing and knowing in accordance with reality |
| yoniso-mānasikāra | wise attention |

# Index

## *About the Authors*

**Sayadaw U Pandita** was the abbot of Panditarama Monastery and Meditation Center in Rangoon, Burma, where he lived. He was a treasured teacher to many students around the world, including Steve Armstrong and Kamala Masters, guiding editors of *Manual of Insight*. He is the author of the classic *In This Very Life: Liberation Teachings of the Buddha.*

**Kate Wheeler** is the author of *Not Where I Started From* and *When Mountains Walked*, and the editor of *In This Very Life* and *Nixon Under the Bodhi Tree and Other Works of Buddhist Fiction*. She lives near Boston.

## *What to Read Next from Wisdom Publications*

**In This Very Life**
*The Liberation Teachings of the Buddha*
Sayadaw U Pandita, Kate Wheeler, and U Aggacitta
Foreword by Joseph Goldstein

"Essential Buddhadhamma from one of the great meditation masters of our time."—Sharon Salzberg

**In the Buddha's Words**
*An Anthology of Discourses from the Pali Canon*
Bhikkhu Bodhi
Foreword by His Holiness the Dalai Lama

"It will rapidly become the sourcebook of choice for both neophyte and serious student alike."—*Buddhadharma*

**Manual of Insight**
*Mahāsi Sayadaw*
*Forewords by Joseph Goldstein and Daniel Goleman*

"It is a great gift to have this translation available."—Sharon Salzberg, author of *Lovingkindness*

**Food for the Heart**
*The Collected Teachings of Ajahn Chah*
Ajahn Chah
Introduction by Ajahn Amaro
Foreword by Jack Kornfield

"This rich collection is a real treasure. Profound, direct, earthy, and often funny, *Food for the Heart* will be especially precious for practitioners of vipassana meditation in all Buddhist lineages."
—Larry Rosenberg, author of *Breath by Breath*

**Emptiness**
*A Practical Guide for Meditators*
Guy Armstrong

"For anyone seeking to understand emptiness, this is a clear and fine guidebook, with precise and practical ways to explore and deepen your practice."—Jack Kornfield, author of *A Path with Heart*

## About Wisdom Publications

Wisdom Publications is the leading publisher of classic and contemporary Buddhist books and practical works on mindfulness. To learn more about us or to explore our other books, please visit our website at wisdompubs.org or contact us at the address below.

Wisdom Publications
199 Elm Street
Somerville, MA 02144 USA

We are a 501(c)(3) organization, and donations in support of our mission are tax deductible.

Wisdom Publications is affiliated with the Foundation for the Preservation of the Mahayana Tradition (FPMT).